Preach It,
Sister!

Preach It, Sister!

Sermons
by
Joanne Reitz Hench

Also by Joanne Reitz Hench

Always Something
A memoir of growing up on a Pennsylvania Dutch Farm

Design by
STICKY EARTH BOOKS

Exton, Pennsylvania
StickyEarth.com

ISBN 979-8-653-16018-9

To Pat Sankus

Acknowledgments

Thank you to the churches which offered me opportunities to preach, and to the pastors who were willing to "share the pulpit" with me.

Thanks to my husband, my children and my grandchildren who encouraged me, offered story lines and advice, listened, shared laughter, and otherwise lent support.

Special gratitude for Annette Raimondi Murray and Sticky Earth Books for helping to bring this book to life, with endless patience and invaluable suggestions.

Table of Contents

Introduction 1

Blessed 3

It's In There 9

Fill Your Lamps 14

Epiphany 19

I Do Choose 25

The Seven Last Words 32

We Know Love by This 38

The Inside of Your Hand 46

Take Off the Graveclothes 54

Story of a Lifetime 57

The Prodigal 63

Theology That Sings 70

Wonderfully Made 75

Seek Ye First 81

Ascension 89

References 97

About the Author 99

Introduction

The sermons in this collection span 20+ years. I was honored to be invited into the pulpit, even while I was working as the music professional in these churches.

The title *Preach It, Sister* is a deliberate choice to honor, not only those who encouraged me along the way, but especially to remember one beloved choir singer. As I climbed into the pulpit one Sunday morning to begin my message, she shouted "Preach it, sister." That brought a smile to everyone's face, and helped to create the positive and relaxed atmosphere I was hoping for. So, to you Pat, now singing with the choirs of angels, I dedicate this work.

The sermons appear in chronological order and are often based on the lessons appointed for that particular Sunday by the 3-Year-Lectionary, common to Roman, Episcopalian and Lutheran Churches. A few exceptions are "the Prodigal," "Wonderfully Made" and "Theology That Sings" in which case I was given free choice as to the topic.

Since these are actually sermons, I suggest that you read them aloud or, at least, slowly and with expression, as might be the style of the one preaching.

The photograph which appears on the back cover was taken in a church in Sitka, Alaska, established by Finnish Lutheran settlers in 1840. Despite fires and demolitions, the pulpit shown here, plus the swallow's nest organ and the painting of Jesus' Transfiguration are all original. These precious items were saved due to the fore-thought, quick action and generosity of the neighboring Presbyterian and Russian Orthodox churches. After the church was restored in the 1960's, the items were returned.

Joanne Reitz Hench
2020

1

Blessed

February 15, 1998
St. Mary's, Middletown DE

SCRIPTURE READINGS: Jeremiah 17:7 ff
Psalm 1
Luke 6:20-49

I had a professor at the seminary who said: "If you can't find the Good News in the Bible, it isn't the fault of the Bible." That's a tough challenge.

So, together, let's walk through the readings for this morning and see if we can find the Good News. Let's see what the writings mean for us today, not simply as abstract comments intended for a foreign time and culture. Let's look for our selves right there in those pages, our selves in the middle of the story.

Do you remember the last time you sneezed and someone automatically responded with "Bless you"? Or you saw a small child do something touching and you mused "Bless her heart." Or someone did something kind for you and you sighed "Bless you." These are all forms of blessing seemingly coming as if by second nature, not requiring much thought.

But how many really meaningful rituals of blessing do we celebrate in our culture? Baptism? Confirmation? Marriage? Gone are the days when couples sought their parents' blessing preceding a marriage proposal.

Our culture today lacks the abundant opportunities for blessing rituals and I think we are the poorer for it. Did you know that one of the oldest scraps of Scripture found and preserved – and the one you will hear at the close of the service today – is the blessing spoken by Moses' brother Aaron:

> *"The Lord bless you and keep you, the Lord make His face to shine upon you, the Lord lift His countenance upon you and give you peace."*

Blessings rituals ought to be front and center in everything we do.

It seems as if a lot of blessing is going on in the Scripture readings this morning. The prophet Jeremiah says:

> *"Blessed are those who trust in the Lord, whose trust is in the Lord. They are like a tree planted by the water...."*

After hearing that, we, the assembly of people responded by reciting Psalm 1:

> *"Happy are those who do not follow the advice of the wicked...They are like trees planted by streams of water, which yield their fruit in due season...They shall prosper in all they do."*

I hope you caught the imagery here. A tree planted by the water will not hunger or thirst. It will be as grounded as we are grounded when fed by the Word of God. We will flourish as the tree flourishes.

Finally we read from the Gospel of Luke where we heard Jesus deliver His Sermon on the Plain. In this passage we have the Blesseds that are commonly called the Beatitudes.

Beatitude comes from the Latin word Beatus which means "exalted joy or happiness."

The word Beata means to bless, to make holy, to invoke divine favor.

Some translators have these Beatitudes read, not "Blessed are you" but "Happy are you."

Happy! You shall be Happy!

I wonder, does this word, or the common concept of this word, go deeply enough? We sometimes over use it: Put on a happy face! Smile, God loves you! Happy faces everywhere – stickers, stamps, advertisements.

Does Happy rest deeply enough in the heart of Jesus' message? We know that Happy is a good thing, right? Jean Houston wrote: "At the height of laughter, the universe is flung into a kaleidoscope of new possibilities."

Was it merely a quest for physical happiness and laughter that brought Jesus down out of the mountain to the plain and kept His listeners enraptured as He spoke? I don't think so.

Spiritually satisfied? Perhaps.

Fundamentally enriched?

Some sources use this translation for beatus "How fortunate for you."

How fortunate for you who are poor, for yours is the Kingdom of Heaven. How fortunate for you who are hungry, who mourn, who are meek...

But why "fortunate?" How does this work?

To whom is Jesus preaching this Sermon on the Plain? The book of Luke was written around 80 to 85 AD. Luke was not an eyewitness to the Christ event, but draws his story from oral accounts (and some written) of those who experienced it firsthand. Each of these Evangelists – Matthew, Mark, Luke and John – wrote for a specific audience. They had an agenda. Luke addresses himself to the Gentiles Christians. In the ancient world, from the Jewish perspective, you were either a Jew or all the rest – Gentiles.

This particular gathering of Gentiles, listening to Jesus' Sermon on the Plain, was an ostracized, non-mainstream group who held the particular position of having left everything and everyone in order to follow Jesus. This crowd REALLY needed to hear some Good News. It had taken a great deal of courage to make that choice, and strength of conviction to hold onto that life. Knowing this helps to bring into focus for us the huge impact Jesus' words had on these people, as He assured them:

> "How fortunate for you. How fortunate for you when people hate you and when they exclude you, revile you, defame you, for surely your reward is great in Heaven."

How fortunate for you.

The Beatitudes that we most commonly hear are from the book of Matthew. Matthew has Jesus speaking to a small, select group up on the Mount where Jesus had retreated to escape the crowds. Matthew has Jesus deliver His blessed – His Beatitudes – in the third person and in the future tense. Blessed are those for they shall be. Luke, on the other hand, has Jesus speaking in the second person and for the present:

> "Blessed are you, for the kingdom is yours."

I had never thought about it that way before. Had you? The effect those small shifts have for me – in this quest to find the Good News, to put ourselves smack in the middle of the story – is that it personalizes the Blesseds for me, for us.

"How fortunate you are". For YOU! Not they. Not someone else. YOU!

"How fortunate you ARE." Not will be; but ARE.

Luke intends his message to be for this time and place. You are already fortunate because you live in the assurance of God's redemptive love through Jesus Christ right now!

And, furthermore, you will be fortunate because you will dwell in that love for all eternity! WOW! How fortunate you are.

Let's focus for a moment on "Blessed are the poor for yours is the kingdom of Heaven." What does this mean? Remember, in finding the Good News, it is wise to put ourselves right in the middle of the story. In this case, we are the poor. I don't think Jesus was referring only to the economically poor. I think He meant the poor as the alienated, the oppressed, the unemployed, the disenfranchised; Those marginalized for a host of reasons; separated, cast aside; the depressed, the stressed, those broken by failed relationships, ostracized because of race, gender, discrimination of all kinds.

Have you found yourself in there somewhere? Blessed are you. How fortunate for you, because Jesus is there, too. Jesus chose the poor. Jesus lived with the poor. This author of Luke represents Jesus as a person begotten of God, appointed, empowered and guided by God, whose task it was to free all people, without distinction, from whatever held them in bondage. Blessed are you; How fortunate for you – you are free.

According to Luke, Jesus announced the purpose of His mission at the very beginning of His ministry by quoting Isaiah 61:

"The Spirit of the Lord is upon me, because
he had anointed me to preach the Good News
to the poor."

The Poor. Are you finding it comforting or problematic to be identified as poor? We come into a situation expecting to minister to, and by some strange and wonderful twist we find ourselves ministered unto instead.

Max Lucado, the beloved Christian author tells a story entitled *A Song in the Dark*. It involves a totally blind man singing boldly and happily on the street corner. People pass not paying much attention. Our storyteller stops and asks if the man has had lunch. The blind singer admits he is hungry and accepts a sandwich. The two sat together chatting between bites. The man was 28 years old, single, living with his parents and 7 brothers.

The writer mused on the differences between them. He himself was an educated and privileged man whose main concerns were thoughts, ideas, people while this man dealt with issues of survival – coins, handouts, food. His clothes were threadbare and torn, his shoes full of holes, and his coat oversized and bulky.

"And still he sang. I wondered which room in his heart that song came from," Lucado says. "Was he singing out of desperation? Out of ignorance?

"No. I decided the motivation that fit his demeanor was one you'd least expect. He was singing from contentment. Somehow, this eyeless pauper had discovered a candle called satisfaction and it glowed in his dark world.

"I looked at the Niagara of faces that flowed past us – grim; professional; some determined; some disguised. But none were singing.

"The irony was painfully amusing. This blind man was the most peaceful person on the street. How many would trade places with him?

"Faith is the bird that sings while it is yet dark.

"Before I helped my friend back to his position on the street, I tried to voice my empathy. Life is hard, isn't it ? A slight smile..... He paused and said 'I'd better get back to work.'

"For almost a block, I could hear him singing. And in my mind's eye, I could see him. But the man I now saw was a different one from the one to whom I'd given a few coins. Though still sightless, he was remarkably insightful. And though I was the one with eyes, it was he who gave me a new vision."

Blessed are you.

How fortunate for you, who are poor, for yours is the kingdom of God.

2

It's In There

February 7, 1999
St. Michael Lutheran, Unionville PA
Scripture Reading: Matthew 5:13ff

There's a term that theologians love to toss around. The word is EXEGISIS. Exegesis – the act of drawing meaning out of a text. Exegesis! It didn't take long for us seminarians to turn that word into another form. We renamed it EXTRA JESUS. Rather fitting, don't you think? Well, we've got Extra Jesus today. I say this because today's Gospel lesson from Matthew, if you read from the New Revised Standard Version, is all in RED. That means, as nearly as scholars can determine, all of this text was actually spoken by Jesus. Jesus' original words! Wow! Now that's a lot of Extra Jesus.

Let's have a look at Matthew 5:13ff. Jesus is continuing His preaching to the disciples gathered on a hillside – the Sermon on the Mount. Jesus says to them:

> *"You are the salt of the earth."*

AND

> *"You are the light of the world."*

Salt and Light. Yes, they are nice and they are convenient to have. But I suspect most of us take them completely for granted. Salt and Light! "Please pass the salt" we might say at the dinner table; "turn off the lights when you leave, please," to conserve electricity; "He's salt of the earth" to compliment someone's dependability.

However, if we examine these commodities in the context of the times and circumstances in which Jesus and His disciples were living, we find that salt and light are far more highly valued than we first might imagine.

Salt was extremely precious and important to those Mediterranean cultures. Yes, it was valued as a seasoning, but even more so for other reasons.

Solutions of salt and water were used to clean and purify everything from homes, to wounds, to food, to fabric. It was a cleaner and a purifier.

In those times with no freezers or ice boxes or canneries, there was no surefire way of keeping meat and vegetables from rotting or spoiling, making them impossible and unhealthy to eat. Solution? Cure these foods with salt. To those ancient cultures, salt was an essential preservative.

Lucrative trade routes were established based on who had salt to exchange and who needed it in order to survive. Availability of salt denoted wealth. It was an important economic necessity.

Taxes were issued and paid in salt.

Furthermore, the primitive Mediterranean religious worshippers brought gifts of salt and grain to their altars as offerings to appease the angry gods.

In our Hebrew history, salt became, because of Its preservative qualities, a symbol of an enduring covenant between God and God's people. The Old Testament book Leviticus 2:13 reads:

> *"You shall not omit from your grain offerings the salt of the covenant with your God; with all your offerings you shall offer salt."*

Today's culture tends to consider salt in more negative terms. We idealize the low-salt or salt-free diet since too much salt can be harmful to our health. Of course, we tend to overindulge in many things.

We say "Take it with a grain of salt" in order to imply that something isn't really all that important.

Or we insult someone by labeling him a "salty character."

If we understand that a society depended on salt to purify, to trade, to make offering to God, to secure promises, to preserve – that food would be not only flavorless, but that it would rot and spoil without salt, so as to be inedible, even lethal – then the words spoken to the disciples, to us "You are the salt of the earth" take on whole new meaning. This is a tremendous responsibility for us. YOU ARE SALT OF THE EARTH. Your life as a Christian calls you into purity of action, preservation of the faith, faithful living, flavoring life with joy and love of Jesus, richness, not just for self, but for all the earth.

YOU ARE SALT OF THE EARTH.

Jesus said "You are...." He didn't say you ought to be OR you should be OR you can be if you try hard enough. He said "You ARE...." You already are. IT'S IN THERE! Because you are of Jesus, created in the image of God, baptized in Jesus, holy because Jesus is holy – by that ownership, that adoption, that association, you already are what Jesus is. You are salt of the earth. IT'S ALREADY IN THERE. Now live it!

Do you remember a commercial years ago, for what product I can't recall, perhaps a spaghetti sauce? The chef would say "It's in there." A friend would ask "But what about....?" The chef's reply "It's in there." "But what about...?" Again "It's in there."

This is what we're saying – because you walk with Jesus, you are what Jesus is. He is salt of the earth, you are salt of the earth. It's already in there.

"You are light of the world." Light! Again, an easy thing to take for granted. Flick a switch or even clap your hands – instant light.

Lighted football fields. Christmas lights. Fireworks displays. Easy. Readily available.

Not so for ancient and primitive cultures who huddled around fires for warmth and protection. Just try to imagine the fire dying out. Total and complete darkness.

In Greek mythology, Prometheus is said to have stolen fire from the gods. For his efforts he suffers eternal punishment.

Consider the northern Europeans during the long dark, winter nights, lighting candles and placing them on a horizontal wagon wheel, longing for the light, for the longer, warmer days to return. This wagon wheel decked with candles became our Advent wreath. It symbolizes our sitting in the darkness, waiting for the light – Jesus – to come.

On a personal level, I think of my days camping, sleeping in a tent in the woods all closed in by airless nylon and vinyl, where I couldn't relax until I had identified that one small point of light in the night sky. That became my reference point. I clung to it.

This is the reality of the absence of light – fear, hunger, longing, dying, no reference point. And what about the metaphor "the darkness of sin?" Sin is darkness – the absence of light.

Jesus says "YOU are the light of the world." YOU signal safety, security, plentitude, warmth, sinlessness, hope, joy, beauty and love. This is a big responsibility!

Jesus says "you ARE." Not should be OR strive to be OR could be OR wanna' be, but ARE. You are the light. It's already in there. How so?

Because you are of Jesus, created in God's image, baptized in Jesus, with Jesus, holy because Jesus is holy – by that association, that covenant, you are what Jesus is "You are the light of the world." It's already in there. Live it!

Today's text reminds me of that old Bible School song "This Little Light of Mine".

In one stanza we'd sing:

"Hide it under a bushel"

and then shout:

"NO!"
I'm gonna' let it shine
Let it shine! Let it shine! All the time!

Jesus went on to say in today's Gospel:

"People don't light a lamp and then put it under
a bowl. Instead, they put it on a stand and
it gives light to the whole house. In the same
way, let your light so shine before people, that
they may see your good deeds and praise your
Father in heaven!"

Let it shine! Let it shine! All the time!

The next time you do something as simple as picking up your salt shaker, or flipping on the light switch, even in that small action, be reminded WHO you are, WHOSE you are. You are salt of the earth. You are light for the world, precisely because you walk with Jesus.

It's in there! Live it!

3

Fill Your Lamps

September 12, 1999
St. Michael Lutheran, Unionville PA

SCRIPTURE READINGS: Matthew 25:1-13
Exodus 3:1-17

Are you ready? I'm sure you have heard that question frequently. Maybe even this morning preparing to leave for church. Are you ready to go back to school? Are you ready for the holiday weekend? Are you ready for Rally Day?

Are you ready?

If you are like me, your stomach lurches a bit at the question. Some of my worst nightmares are about not being prepared for some occasion. Usually those nightmares have me at the organ, the whole congregation is waiting patiently, and I can't find the music, or the hymnal, or my organ shoes. Or God forbid, in an unfamiliar setting, I can't even find the organ!

Today's Gospel from Matthew, in the NRSV Bible, bears the heading "The fate of the unprepared." Sounds ominous, doesn't it?

Now that I've stirred up your anxieties, let's see if I can ease them with a message of hope, assurance, encouragement, a little Good News that will keep you excited, hopefully, but not stressed.

In Matthew 25:1-13, Jesus is telling a story as He so often does. He chooses a topic with which the people could easily identify. Light! In Jesus' time, long before electricity, how did the people keep their homes lighted? Oil lamps. How did they keep the oil lamps ready to be lit? By keeping them filled with oil. They had to constantly refill the lamps with oil, so that any time light was required, the lamps could be lighted. If they were caught with their lamps empty, they may be left sitting alone in the dark. Furthermore, in those days in a small village in Palestine, it was against the law to be in the street at night without a lamp.

When a couple was to be married, the whole village was invited to join the celebratory procession through the streets. Bridesmaids carried the brightly lit lamps to greet the groom and to accompany the bridal couple. The celebrating lasted for days. If a bridesmaid missed the procession because she had taken time to run somewhere to buy oil, because she was unprepared, she would most likely miss the celebration. The door of the bridal chamber would be closed and she could not enter. She would be left alone.

This is no synthetic story that Jesus uses for His message, but a real slice of life from a village in Palestine.

This reading from Matthew is often appointed for the time in November just before Advent. We call that time "The last days." The last days before what? Before Jesus' Advent? Before Jesus' Second Coming? Before the last judgement?

The last days?

You see, at the time Jesus was telling this story, He is on His way to Jerusalem and the people are following Him there. He tells them that, in Jerusalem, He will be handed over to be crucified, but that He will:

"Come again in Glory and all the angels with Him."

Jesus wants the people to know that He WILL return and that they should be ready, should be prepared. Like the wise maidens in the story, their lamps need to be filled with oil, ready to be lighted for the joyful celebration. Get yourself ready. In other words, turn back to God, fortify those souls for Jesus' coming. Be prepared. Fill those lamps with oil, or you will miss out and be left alone in the dark.

The story of the wise and foolish maidens carries at least two universal warnings. The first one is: There are certain things that cannot be obtained at the very last minute. For example, it is far too late for a student to be cramming when the day of the exam has come. Proper preparation is done over time with much review and repetition. The second universal warning is: There are certain things that cannot be borrowed. The foolish maidens found it impossible to borrow oil from the wise maidens when the bridegroom appeared, and they discovered their lamps were empty. Just the same, a person cannot borrow a relationship with God; a person cannot borrow character. A person must be clothed in it.

As always, when I reflect on a portion of the scriptures, I ask myself "Where am I in this story? Am I the foolish one who was caught unprepared? Am I the wise one with enough oil? Would I be willing to share it? Or am I the merchant with enough oil to supply everyone – at the right price?" I think we won't go there today. There's another whole sermon or two in those questions.

All of this now having been said, the very large-scale, dramatic lack of preparedness for a major event – Jesus' second coming; the Day of Judgement; our meeting face-to-face with God – I would like to take time to make a case for the less dramatic, the more ordinary, the everyday ministries for which we are called to be prepared.

Each of us is called through our Baptism to minister in four main areas: family, community, church, and occupation. Family; Community; Church; Occupation.

As we move though each day, opportunities for witness, for compassion, for forgiveness, for mercy, for setting a good example present themselves. Are we ready to BE in that moment, Christ-like? Are we programmed to ask ourselves in that moment "What would Jesus do?" Are we fortified to be everyday disciples? Are our lamps filled with oil and ready to light the darkness?

Perhaps, at this point you are wondering, how is it exactly that we fill those lamps and keep them filled, ready to burn and give off light? How do we fortify for everyday discipleship?

We know how to fortify our physical selves for healthy living. We eat good food, get adequate rest, take vitamins, exercise, indulge in no excesses.

In the same way we fortify our spiritual selves. We pray unceasingly, we read God's Word and we gather here with this community of believers.

The Christian community comes together where we hold and build each other up. If you think about it, Jesus always says:

"Come, gather round. Come hear the story.
Come you who are weary and I will give
you rest."

And then He says:

"Go. Go and do likewise. Go and sin no more.
Go and preach and teach and baptize."

I have a favorite children's sermon I like to preach – my M & M Sermon. M & M - Meal and Mission. We gather together to hear the Word, to commune around the Table, and we pray and listen and respond and take our meal together. In that way we are spiritually fortified so that we can GO and do our mission in the world. Meal and Mission. COME. And then GO.

Fill your lamps, fortify your Spirit for everyday discipleship. Look at Moses from today's Old Testament lesson. Moses has his famous encounter with the burning bush. The bush was burning but was not consumed. That's LIGHT for you! And from the bush the voice of God commands Moses to go to Pharaoh and tell him:

"Let my people go."

Now there was a real opportunity for everyday discipleship, don't you think?

What did Moses do? He responded:

> *"But who am I*
> *that you would ask me to do this?"*

And God answered:

> *"I will be with you"*

I will be with you.

With that assurance we are fortified, we are ready, we are prepared. Our lamps are filled, ready to give off light. God's light in the world through everyday discipleship.

In a few moments we will respond by singing the hymn *Christ Be Our Light*. Before we do, let me highlight a few significant phrases.

> *"Longing for light, we wait in darkness...*
> *Your Word alone has power to save us.*
> *Make us your living voice...*
> *Make us your bread, broken for others...*
> *Make us your building, sheltering others,*
> *walls made of living stone...*
> *Christ be our light! Shine in our hearts."*

Come. Fill your lamps. Pray. Listen to God's Word. Come together around the table. Be fortified.

Then Go. Be a lamp lighted for the world to see.

Amen.

4

Epiphany

January 23, 2000
St. Michael Lutheran, Unionville PA

SCRIPTURE READINGS: Jonah 3:1-5
Mark 1:1-14

E piphany! We are in the middle of the Epiphany season. Epiphany! What do we do with Epiphany?

We just came through the Christmas season. We know what to do with that — all the rituals and the customs, decorations and parties. We know how to sing all the beautiful carols and how to exchange gifts.

But what about Epiphany? Have you baked your Epiphany cookies? Did you put up your Epiphany tree? Are the kids coming home for Epiphany? Have you done your Epiphany shopping? These questions don't roll off the tongue very smoothly.

What do we do with Epiphany?

Only a few weeks ago we were gathered around a tiny baby in a manger, and we were singing "Glory to God in the Highest" adoring God's gift to us in the form of a son — God made flesh.

The Eastern Church celebrates Christmas on the date of the

Epiphany, January 6th, with the visit of the three wisemen. Yet, just three days later our Scripture readings have us beside the Jordan River where John is baptizing an adult Jesus, a man now of about age 30.

Epiphany! It is a season that seems somehow out of sorts. To many Christians in the West it is like a misplaced Christmas.

The word Epiphany comes from the Greek epiphanos, which means revelation or manifestation. Epiphany is the time when God reveals God's self to the world in the person of Jesus Christ. This is the time when we see and hear all the good stuff about our God through the man Jesus.

How does Jesus reveal Himself and the God whom He represents, the God who He is? Think of some of the great stories we read during this season. There's the wedding at Cana where Jesus performs His first miracle, changing water into wine. He reads to the elders and scribes in the temple at age twelve. He wanders and preaches and teaches and performs healing miracles. He is baptized in the Jordan and the heavens open up and the voice of God says:

"This is my beloved Son in whom I am
well pleased."

These are all stories about who God is through Jesus.

Throughout the season, shining through all of these revelations is the symbol of Light.

"Arise, shine for your light has come,"

says Isaiah.

"The men who walked in darkness have seen
a great light."

The three wisemen followed a star, the most famous symbol of Light, to see the baby in a manger bed.

During the season of Advent, we lighted candles to symbolize our waiting in the darkness for the Light to come. Jesus the Light, the brightest Morningstar. Light!

Light is wonderful. We prefer light to darkness. We are scared and lonely in the dark. We sit huddled in the dark waiting for the light to come.

However, the problem is, that when the light comes, it reveals to us things we may not want to see.

Let me draw an analogy. Suppose you want to serve a meal to invited guests. Well, your tablecloth is a little threadbare, your house is a little dusty, your dinnerware is old and well-used. Your hair doesn't look the greatest and you have put on a few pounds. All of this could be embarrassing. So, what's the solution? Have a candlelight dinner. Perfect. All these flaws can be well disguised by the softness of candlelight.

Suppose that right in the middle of all this pleasantness, someone turns on the lights. What happens? The flaws are revealed. You have been caught in your disguise.

Likewise, the world, though longing for the light, was rather comfortable wallowing in the darkness of their sin. But into that darkness came Jesus Christ, the one true Light. That's good! But what Jesus also did was reveal to the world their own sin. It was embarrassing, uncomfortable and very difficult to accept.

So where is this Jesus, this light, revealing Himself in our readings this morning? He is in Galilee, Mark tells us, proclaiming the Good News from God and saying:

> *"The time is fulfilled, and the kingdom of*
> *God has come near; repent and believe*
> *in the Good News."*

So, Jesus has taken up John the Baptist's mode of preaching. He is calling for repentance.

To whom is Jesus revealing Himself?

> *"As Jesus passes along the Sea of Galilee, he sees*
> *Simon and his brother Andrew casting a net*
> *into the sea, for they were fishermen."*

Fishermen were not people of great wealth or education or social stature. They were hard workers. There were nets to be repaired constantly, and, whether the fishermen stood on the side of the water to cast their nets, or rode in the boats to drag their nets to catch fish, they were constantly in motion. We cannot imagine that they were simply lounging by the side of the water sharing fish stories about great catches. They were busy. Into this active, busy scene came Jesus and said:

"Follow me."

Amazing as it seems, they immediately dropped their nets and followed after Jesus.

This immediacy is in direct contrast with the reaction of Jonah in our Old Testament reading today. Now there's a "fish story" for you! Remember when God called to Jonah and said:

"Go to Nineveh and tell those people that if they do not mend their ways, they and their entire city will be destroyed."

How did Jonah answer the call? He hopped into a boat and fled in the opposite direction. There was no way Jonah was going to Nineveh to deliver bad news. He ran from God's call.

Jonah was a very reluctant prophet. So, what happened? A storm brewed, the seas got rougher and rougher and Jonah was asleep in the hold. The pagan sailors, having failed to appease their gods, figured it must be Jonah's God who was causing the trouble. They dragged Jonah out of bed and tossed him into the sea. Along came a big fish, a whale according to some translators, and swallowed Jonah. (God's way of saying "Now that I've got your attention!")

After about three days inside the big fish, Jonah had a change of heart and decided to heed God's call and travel to Nineveh. Sure enough, the fish spewed Jonah forth onto the shore, and that is where our "fish story" picked up today. Jonah went to Nineveh, delivered God's warning and the people changed their ways. Seeing this change, God spared the city from destruction.

The common thread that I see between this wonderful Old Testament fish story and the New Testament account of Jesus calling "Follow me," is that there is *change*. Jonah changed his mind. The people of Nineveh repented and changed. God changed His mind and saved the city. And by the Sea of Galilee, the fishermen changed their lives forever. They dropped their nets and followed Jesus.

These fisherman, Simon, James and Andrew were ordinary folk, but they were chosen for no ordinary task. Jesus in His call was saying:

"Come. Follow me, and I will reveal God to you.
Then, it will be your job to reveal God to others.
I will make you fishers of men."

Max Lucado, in his book *God Came Near*, writes, "I have a feeling some of you can relate to the call. You've been called to go out on a limb a time or two. We know the kind of fellow who goes out on a limb. Radical. Extremist. Liberal. Always going overboard. Always stirring the leaves. The stable ones are the ones who know how to stay close to home and leave well enough alone. You know the imbalance of having one foot in your will and one foot in God's. You know too well the butterflies that swarm in the pit of your stomach when you realize change is in the air."

Perhaps changes are in the air right now. Maybe you are in the midst of making a decision. It's disrupting. You've grown comfortable in your place. Then you hear the call:

"Come. Follow me."

Take a stand. Move. Forgive. Evangelize. Sacrifice.

Faith is a verb. A verb implies action – a beginning action and a continuing action. God calls; we answer. God reveals; we repent. We change. We follow. We get inspired. We reveal God to others. We tell "fish stories" with great enthusiasm. We grow discouraged sometimes. God builds us up. God reveals some more. We continue.

Even though I use the term "fish stories," this does not imply that they are untrue. Each time fish stories are told, they are embellished a bit. The teller is so excited about his experience, he can't help but report with abundant enthusiasm. That's not a bad thing. In calling the disciples and us to be fishers of men, Jesus is asking these fishermen to tell fish stories with great enthusiasm. Stories so unimaginably great, that you almost can't believe them to be true.

We talk about Jonah being swallowed by a whale, and my logical, human mind says, "No. That's not possible. All those digestive juices and all that time without any oxygen. He couldn't possibly survive." But my mind of faith says, "God has the power to do whatever God wants to do." And then my imagination is excited by the unlimited possibilities that mind of faith allows.

Have you noticed that all of these stories begin with God taking the initiative? God approaches us to voice the call. God spoke to Jonah, asking him to go to Nineveh. God, in Jesus, came down to the seashore and spoke to the fishermen. Listen to these words from our beloved hymn *Lord You Have Come to the Lakeshore*:

> *"You have come down to the lakeshore,*
> *seeking neither the wise nor the wealthy,*
> *But only asking for me to follow.*
> *Sweet Lord, you have looked into my eyes,*
> *Kindly smiling, you've called out my name.*
> *On the sand I have abandoned my small boat;*
> *Now with you, I will seek other seas."*

So, then what do we do with Epiphany? We listen. We remain open to revelation. We answer the call. We follow.

5

I Do Choose

February 13, 2000
St. Michael Lutheran, Unionville PA

SCRIPTURE READINGS: 2 Kings 5:1-14
Mark 1:40-45

I went shopping the other day in Border's Bookstore. We had received a gift certificate for Christmas and this seemed like a good time to redeem it. As I browsed through the shelves, I very much had today's readings on my mind. I began to count, just out of curiosity, the number of books on health, healing or anything related to those subjects. I was amazed! Listen to this. On the subject of General and Family Health, I counted 360 titles; Medical Reference, 400 titles; Nutrition, 200 titles; Alternative Medicine, 480; and, get this, Self-Help, 2100.

One of the main debate issues in political campaigns is the cost of health care. Biotech stocks are gaining a lot of clout on Wall Street as we gain momentum on gene research and therapy, and develop countless drugs for healing. It is all around us. We find ourselves saying "I don't have a lot of money, but I have my health." What we read, what we vote for and what we invest in shows a real preoccupation with matters of health.

As I read all the Gospel passages from Mark for the 8 Sundays in this Epiphany season, I discovered that 5 out of the 8 are stories of Jesus performing healing miracles. What does this mean? Does it mean that the times and culture made those people unusually unhealthy? Or that the writer of the Gospel was somehow obsessed with illness? That the miracle of healing somehow proved that Jesus really was who He claimed to be?

I don't believe the frequency of healing stories means any of those things. I think this is real life, this strong concern about being and staying disease-free. It was as true then as it is now.

We live in a kind of continuous Angst, because somewhere deep down we are aware, that no matter how well we eat, exercise, take vitamins, pray and meditate, that our health is still a fragile thing and can change in literally a heartbeat. Without good health all other areas of our lives are adversely affected. Even more so, in Jesus time, before modern medicine, how frightening it must have been to trust a healer with limited resources who probably used mantras, perhaps oil, maybe a few herbs and spices. Stories of healing, then, would be a big deal and worthy of telling and retelling.

Our Gospel reading says that a leper came to Jesus begging Him and kneeling:

"If you choose, you can make me clean,"

In the Old Testament text we read:

"Naaman, commander of the army of the king of Aram...though a mighty warrior, suffered from leprosy."

Both of these men wanted desperately to be healed.

Leprosy was a terrible disease. At its worst it claimed skin, fingers and toes and ultimately meant an agonizing death. Leprosy was a commonly used term for a variety of skin ailments. We might call them names like psoriasis, Rosacea, or even prickly heat. Some were curable. Some were not. Any such skin malady rendered the sufferer unclean and so he was banished from the community. The leper not only endured the physical disease, but he had to bear the mental, emotional and spiritual anguish of being completely alienated from human society.

In every case, a ritual washing was ordered, followed by an inspection done by officials within the synagogue. In the Old Testament lesson, the prophet Elisha told Naaman to go wash 7 times in the Jordan river and he would be healed. Naaman received his miracle even though he was not a believer up to that point. Likewise, the leper in the Gospel of Mark, begging:

"If you choose you can make me clean"

got his healing miracle. Vs 41 - Moved with pity, Jesus stretched out His hand and touched him and said:

"I do choose. Be made clean."

Immediately the leprosy left Him and he was made clean. And then Jesus said:

"Go show yourself to the priest, and offer yourself for your cleansing as Moses commanded."

There never has been any disease that so separated a person from his fellow men as leprosy did. And this leper was the man Jesus touched! First and foremost, Jesus' reaction was compassion. Jesus reached out His hand and touched the leper. The medical knowledge of the day would have said that Jesus was running a terrible risk of contracting a deadly infection. But Jesus stretched out His hand and touched him. This is to show that the true Christian will break any convention and will take any risk to help a brother or sister in need.

Are we to believe that the healing power is in the water? Was it the water in the Jordan river that healed Naaman? Was it the water in the synagogue washing ritual that made the leper clean? No. It was the power of God's love that took an ordinary element – water – and used it to work the miracle. Just so, it is in the waters of our Baptism, this earthly element, that cleanses us, heals us, empowers us through God's love in Christ.

The more I tried to make this message about physical healing, the more it wanted to be about all types of healing. That is the Spirit at work and I had to pay attention. What about those times when we pray for physical healing and we don't receive it? Our disease rages on and our faith falters because we believe our prayers are not being heard. What about those times? How is it that Jesus seems to say "I do choose; be made clean" to some people and not to others? We feel like the small child, last to be chosen for the team - "Why didn't they pick me?"

There are two things about healing miracles that we need to consider.

1) Do we really recognize miracles when they occur?

2) Are you open to and praying for miracles that are not for physical healing, but for healing of the mind and spirit.

When I visit the Lutheran Deaconess Community in Gladwyne and pray with the sisters there, they have taught me something. Their prayers always go this way:

> *"We ask for healing for all those who suffer in body, mind and spirit."*

What does this mean? For the writer of the Gospel of Mark:

> *"...healing stands for the restored wholeness of the individual. Health is the manifestation of God's Kingdom; the way humans were intended to be by the loving God who created them."*

> (*Woman's Bible Commentary*, Mary Ann Tolbert)

Disease and illness alienate the sick ones from the community. Healing restores them to full fellowship in the community. When we are healed in mind and spirit, through the forgiveness of our sins, through the waters of Baptism, we are restored to full fellowship with the community AND to the loving God who created us. Then, physical illness and death have no power over us. We can dwell securely in the safety assured by the healing waters.

Are we able to accept that form of healing? Can we accept that mind/spirit is real healing, a restoration to God and community?

Let me tell you about Martha. Martha was a longtime friend of mine. She had sung in the choir in a former parish where I served as Music Director/Organist. Martha lived her faith every day. She loved, accepted and nurtured everyone, simply because that is what a faithful Christian does. I loved her. She laughed at my jokes, with a wonderful, throaty mirth that rumbled up from deep inside her considerable girth. Several years ago, Martha developed cancer. She fought for a long time, participating in all the treatments that conventional medicine had to offer at the time. She continued to pray for healing. She attended healing services and was anointed with oil. Her physical condition deteriorated. She quit singing in the choir and ultimately could no longer attend church services.

In one of my conversations with her, she spoke about a visit to friends in Virginia, where she sat by a waterfall and, while praying, was filled with an enormous sense of peace and safety and well-being. Fascinating – there's that cleansing water imagery again. She admitted that every time she became afraid, she concentrated on that time at the waterfall, trying to regain those feelings of peace.

Martha died that October. Shortly before her death I sat with her. We reminisced, we sang, we prayed for a safe journey and I asked her "How do you feel?" She answered "I'm excited!"

Was this a healing miracle. Yes, it certainly was. Maybe not the physical healing we asked for, but certainly healing of the mind and spirit. Was my spirit healed that day through her witness of faith. Yes, it was.

"I'm excited" she said.

In the hymn *There is a Balm in Gilead* the words

> *".... To heal the sin-sick soul"*

come to mind. What exactly makes our souls sin-sick? What is our sin?

Our sin is anything that separates us from God. That can be many things – broken relationships, depression, addiction, obsession – when something else has become our god.

What is the balm that heals the sin-sick soul? Grace. Grace through faith through Jesus Christ.

God always says:

> *"I do choose; be made clean."*

In the waters of Baptism we are chosen, healed, brought back to the community, protected, made safe and secure.

Hildegard von Bingen in the 12th Century wrote these words:

> *"Under your protection, I rejoice, O God!*
> *In your shadow, I exult, O God!*
> *You rescue me from the heaviness of sin*
> *My soul anticipates drawing ever closer to you...*
> *Beckons me come under your protection*
> *Into the shadow of your power.*
> *I am secure from all enemies there."*

My prayer for us today is that we receive the healing for which we pray, healing of body, mind and spirit, healing for our sin-sick souls, and that we recognize it when it comes.

From the hymn *Thy Holy Wings*:

> *"Oh, wash me in the waters of Noah's*
> *cleansing flood.*
> *Give me a willing spirit, a heart both kind*
> *and good.*

Oh, take me into thy keeping all creatures
great and small
And while they sweetly slumber, enfold us
one and all."

Amen!

6

The Seven Last Words

February 27, 2000
St. Michael Lutheran, Unionville PA
SCRIPTURE READINGS: Hosea 2:14-23
Mark 2:13-22

The congregation of a small country church was discussing the possible purchase of a new chandelier. Most were enthusiastic, but one man held out.

"I have three reasons for objecting," he said. "First, nobody here knows how to spell the word, so we couldn't order one. Second, even if we got one, there's nobody here who knows how to play it. Third, if we could come up with the money, I say what we really need is a new light fixture."

Clearly this story is about change and the fear of trying something new. Have you heard of the Seven Last Words of the Church?

"We've never done it that way before."

Jesus was something new! If you remember, during this time, this Epiphany, Jesus was about the business of revealing who He was. He wandered around Nazereth, Capurnaum, the Sea of Galilee calling for followers, teaching, preaching and working miracles.

Everywhere He went, He was constantly stalked by a group of suspicious scribes and Pharisees. They watched and scrutinized, hoping to catch Jesus in some indiscretion, some infraction of their countless laws, some nasty faux pas so they could say "Aha! WE knew it! He's a fraud."

"Why is He teaching with such authority? How can He cast out demons? Where does He get the right to heal the sick? Only God can do that." These were some of the comments in the stories we have read over the past few weeks. Now today, in this Gospel lesson, Jesus has chosen to sit at table and eat with tax collectors and sinners. Maybe His stalkers had finally caught Him.

Jesus was new on the scene in ancient Israel. We think we have an inkling of who Jesus is, but who were these Pharisees, and why were they so concerned about Jesus and His behavior? Why were they so quick to say "We've never done it this way before"?

The Pharisees were a Jewish religious party who had wide influence in the Holy Land. They were scholars who studied the Torah and determined how the written law should be carried out. They were particularly rigid about the rules concerning the Sabbath, ritual washing and practices involving food. The Pharisees held a lot of power in the synagogues and were interested in holding onto that power. The new man, Jesus, by the way He conducted Himself, challenged their power at every turn. They didn't like it. You might say the Pharisees were so caught up in the letter of the law that they had lost the spirit of the law. They had forgotten about common people and had created an elitist society. Sound familiar?

What was so scandalous about Jesus' choice of dining companions? In today's Gospel, we read:

> *"And as He sat at dinner in Levi's house, many tax collectors and sinners were also sitting with Jesus and His disciples - for there were many who followed Him."*

Tax collectors and sinners! Interesting. We know that Levi, sometimes called Matthew, was a tax collector. Tax collectors were appointed by the Romans to collect taxes from the citizens and from the merchants passing through town. Most tax collectors grossly overcharged and, consequently, became more and more wealthy. They were despised by the Jews for their reputation for cheating, and for their support of Rome.

Jesus was new! He sat at table with some of the most despised and rejected people of the time – tax collectors and sinners. Jesus knew that this was where His message of love and forgiveness was most needed, right there in the midst of sin and greed. So that is where He seated Himself.

The Pharisees were infuriated. "Why does He eat with tax collectors and sinners?" they asked. We've never done it that way before.

What Jesus was doing in choosing to associate with those that were outcast or unacceptable, was very radical, very revolutionary for that time. Remember the lepers and the lame man in previous Gospel accounts? In His response to those who needed healing, and His willingness to let social events be interrupted by requests for healing, even from NON-BELIEVERS, Jesus was showing a new way.

It is simple to sit here comfortably 2000 years later and pass judgement on those Pharisees. But as always, we must ask ourselves the question, "Where am I in this story?" Who are the tax collectors and sinners that I reject and despise and consider unfit to be at my table? Who are the ones I am afraid to associate with because they are poor, or diseased of different in color, race, creed, gender? Where and when is it that I say "But we've never done it that way before."

A few weeks ago, while driving on Naaman's Road in North Wilmington, I glanced at a church displaying this sign:

"CHALLENGED BY FAITH; GUIDED BY LOVE."

Now there's sermon material, I thought, and meditated on it for weeks afterward. "Challenged by faith; guided by love." Jesus was new. He showed us a new way. He put Himself right in the middle of the rejected and the despised and ate with them, and by so doing, challenged the faith of everyone, especially those pesky Pharisees. He showed these outcasts love and compassion. This is God in Jesus, willing to place God's self, right in the middle of our sin and show us love and compassion.

Are we comfortable? Is ours a comfortable faith? Are we satisfied with the rules and with maintaining the status quo? Can we be challenged by our faith and trust that we are being guided by God?

Some of the strongest words we use in declaring who we are as Christians, and what our mission is in the world, are contained in the hymns that we sing. Consider what would happen though if we forgot to be challenged by faith and guided by love, forgot how to be new in Jesus Christ's example, forgot how to declare our faith and our mission. We might become God's frozen people as featured in a recent article in *Grace Notes*. This article, entitled *The Lukewarm Church*, announces a publication of church songs whose titles were chosen because, and I quote, "we didn't want to turn anyone off with threatening words. People in today's society get kind of uncomfortable with too much talk about commitment and dedication."

Contents include:

Amazing Grace, How Interesting the Sound
All Hail the Suggestion of Jesus' Name
Blest Be the Tie That Doesn't Cramp My Style
I Lay My Inappropriate Behaviors on Jesus
I'm Fairly Certain That My Redeemer Lives
Take My Life and Let Me Be
A Comfy Mattress Is Our God

As I surveyed resource material to prepare this message, I came across one writer who said "The preacher will look hard and long to find the clever thread that ties these readings (Hosea 2:14-23 & Mark 2:13-22) together." At first glance, the Old Testament reading from Hosea and this one from Mark seem to have little in common. But with closer scrutiny, that clever thread began to materialize for me. Everything in Hosea 2:14 ff talks about making things new.

> *"I will remove the names of Baal from her mouth;*
> *I will abolish the bow, the sword and war from*
> *the land; I will make you lie down in safety;*
> *I will take you for my wife forever; I will take*
> *you as my wife in faithfulness."*

You see, Hosea was one in a long line of prophets sent to Israel. Most of these prophets brought a message of judgement from a wrathful and angry God. But Hosea was different. His message always reflected a faithful and loving God, whose only desire was to return Israel to a life of faith and love for her God. This God had forgiven Israel's waywardness many times and would continue to do so, because God loved God's people.

Hosea was the perfect choice to deliver this message to Israel because he, himself was married to a woman named Gomer who was repeatedly unfaithful to him; and yet he forgave her and took her back again and again *because he loved her.* This explains Hosea's use of the marriage language. God said to Israel (and it might be Hosea talking to his wife Gomer),

> *"I will take you for my wife in justice, in*
> *steadfast love, in mercy and in faithfulness."*

This is new! This is different! God depicted as faithful and loving, like a groom with his new bride, rather than God depicted as wrathful and angry and judgmental.

This is new, just as Jesus' conduct is new to the judgmental and legalistic Pharisees.

Jesus always knew just how to tell a story or draw a parallel to make His message clearer, always using examples from real life that were familiar to His listeners. To respond to the Pharisees' criticism, Jesus said "...no one puts new wine into old wineskins; otherwise the wine will burst the skins; but one puts new wine into fresh wineskins."

Wineskins would have been a very familiar item to the Israelites. They were made from goatskin sewn together at the edges. When these skins were new, they had a certain elasticity; as they grew older, they became hard and unyielding. New wine, when it was put into the wineskins, was still fermenting; it gave off gasses which would cause expansion and pressure. If the wineskin was new, it would expand and yield to the pressure, but if it was old and hard and dry, it would explode, and the wine and skin and everything would be lost.

Jesus was new! He came with a message that was startlingly different; Jesus was challenging the faith of those who had been, up to this time, the interpreters and keepers of the law. Jesus urged them to be like new wineskins, able to expand and understand that the love of God is for all, not just a chosen and acceptable few.

Who are the despised and rejected in our world? Addicts? Those with AIDS? Those whose skin is a different color? Immigrants? Those with mental and emotional illness?

Who are the elitist, legalistic Pharisees? The church? We ourselves? White Anglo-Saxon Protestants? U.S. citizens?

Beware the Last Seven Words of the Church: "We've never done it this way before." Hear the Word, the Good News. See this new Jesus. Let yourself be challenged by faith and guided by love. Be the new wineskin, letting the new wine of Jesus' example bubble and expand within you, in that wineskin, and thus, create new excitement in your life of faith and in your witness to others.

7

We Know Love by This

May 14, 2000
St. Michael Lutheran, Unionville PA
SCRIPTURE READINGS: Acts 4:5-12
Psalm 2
I John 3:16-24
John 10:11-18

St. John's is a small German Lutheran church in Leck Kill, a Pennsylvania Dutch farming community about three hours north of here in Northumberland County. My parents were married there, my siblings and I were baptized and confirmed there. It was in that church that I first played for congregational hymn-singing at the age of 9, and began my career as a church music professional at the age of 15. It was at St. John's most recently that family and community gathered twice within the last year to celebrate the lives of my parents, and then lay them to rest in the adjoining church yard. St. John's is my home church. It is a part of me. It is woven into the fabric of who I am as a spiritual being..

There's a big, beautiful stained-glass window on the back wall of St. John's, the wall facing the road so all can see it. It is a picture of Jesus, one hand holding His shepherd's staff and the other cuddling a cute, tiny, helpless lamb to His chest. I can't say that I stood still and gazed for long periods of time at that window. I was busy growing up, and was always on the move. But I knew that it was there. It was comforting to me. Even today when I envision that window, I feel calm.

"I am the Good Shepherd."

Today is Good Shepherd Sunday. It is the 4th Sunday OF Easter not AFTER Easter. We are still worshipping in the glow of the resurrection experience. On this day each year, we traditionally hear all of those wonderful texts about Jesus as the Good Shepherd. The Pslamody is always number 23:

> *"The Lord is my shepherd, I shall not want.*
> *He leads me beside still waters;*
> *He restores my soul."*

The Gospel says to us today.

> *"I am the Good Shepherd.*
> *The good shepherd lays down his life for his sheep.*
> *I am the Good Shepherd.*
> *I know my own and my own know me."*

The Word is very rich today. Some of our most familiar and beloved texts are heard. In the First Letter of John we read:

> *"We know love by this, that Jesus Christ laid*
> *down His life for us. Little children, let us love,*
> *not in word or in speech, but in truth and action."*

Today is also Mother's Day. Happy Mother's Day to all of you.

With all of this – the good shepherd, the talk of love, of laying down your life, this celebration of loving mothers on Mother's Day – it would be a great temptation to get very sentimental. Don't get me wrong. There's nothing wrong with sentiment. I can shed a tear as well as the next person. However, I believe I would do a great disservice to the richness of the Word today, if I settled for mere sentiment. As always, let's dig a little deeper; let's stay well-grounded in the Word. You will not be getting a Hallmark greeting card sermon this morning.

Let's go back to that stained glass window at St. John's and the cute little lamb cuddled in Jesus' arms. St. John's, Leck Kill, is in the heart of farming country. I was raised on one of those farms. Here is "the rest of the story" as Paul Harvey used to say. The truth is, sheep are not always cute and cuddly! Farm animals are dirty and smelly and, sometimes, not very smart. In their greed at feeding time, they will actually trample on each other. They stick their heads into the trough, so that whatever you are trying to pour in there, spills all over their heads. I helped to clean more animal pens than I care to remember. My siblings and I would wear kerchiefs tied over our nose and mouth to keep out the odor. It wasn't much help. As my mother milked the cows, she would make sure the cow's tail was fastened to the side of the stall, or else, dear Elsie would swish that tail repeatedly over mother's face and head. Not a very cute picture, is it? Have I managed to ruin all the warm fuzzies we felt a few moments ago?

Seeing Jesus in that window, cuddling a cute little lamb took some imagination for me. The metaphor – Jesus as the Good Shepherd, cuddling me, as a cute little lamb – that worked for me only if I deliberately forgot the other "stuff", the dirt, the smell and the greed. Wait though. The other "stuff" serves to make the metaphor all the richer. Am I, are we, the sheep of God's pasture, always cute and cuddly? Aren't we sometimes greedy, jealous, mean, dirty, smelly, not too smart, wandering away from God our shepherd?

And yet, despite all of that, God continues to love us, bring us home, hold us close to His heart.

"I am the Good Shepherd. We know love by this."

Life is messy. We do not always walk in green pastures, or rest beside still waters. There is famine and war and flood. The world seems more like a place of lost souls than restored souls. We trample on each other in our greed for wealth. We clog our cities, our skies, our lungs with air that is fouled by the sin of uncaring.

We are not always lovable and we know it. What a gift, then, to hear those words from John's letter:

> *"We know love by this, that He laid down*
> *His life for us."*

We know love by this, that despite everything, we are loved. An old hymn has these words in one verse:

> *"Perverse and foolish oft I've strayed, and yet*
> *in love He sought me. And gently on His*
> *shoulders laid, home rejoicing brought me."*

Mothers, on this Mother's Day, you can certainly resonate with this. And when I say mothers, I mean fathers, as well. All parents. In spite of everything, we love our children, and would literally lay down our lives for them.

It really wasn't until I became a mother that I understood what that meant to "lay down your life" for someone. To sacrifice! You sacrifice your waistline, maybe, or a good night's sleep, or privacy in the bathroom. Way beyond those things, when you become a parent you realize, for the first time in your life, there is something – this child, this precious lamb – for whom you would sacrifice your own life.

If that child were facing surgery, you would gladly climb onto the table and take his/her place. If they were drowning or trapped in a burning building, you would throw yourself into the water, or into the flames to rescue them, without a thought for your own safety.

> *"We know love by this, that Jesus Christ laid*
> *down His life for us - and we ought to lay*
> *down our lives for each other."*

In his book *The Courage To Love*, William Sloane Kauffman writes:

> *"It is not because we have value that we are loved, but because we are loved that we have value."*

Again

> *"It is not because we have value that we are loved, but because we are loved that we have value."*

With the love of the Good Shepherd as our example, this incredible, unconditional love that gives us value, we are charged and moved to do likewise. Because we know that we are valued, we can do nothing less than act for others as the Good Shepherd acted for us.

What does this mean? That we should go around trying to die for someone to prove how loving we are? Probably for most of us, the possibilities for this will not be as dramatic as plunging ourselves into frigid water, or tossing ourselves into a burning building, or donating a kidney. Listen to verse 17 in John's letter:

> *"How does God's love abide in anyone who has the world's goods and sees a brother or sister in need and yet refuses to help?"*

That verse makes clear for us the nature of laying down our lives for others. It is to serve those in need. "We KNOW love by this" and so we SHOW love by this. Not dying for others, but living for others. It is far easier to SAY you would die for someone than it is to actually LIVE for that person.

John goes on to say:

> *"Little children, let us love, not in word and speech, but in truth and action."*

Love is a verb. Love is an action word. This love action can take many forms – building a school in Nicaragua, giving food to the Food Pantry, volunteering at the hospital, delivering meals to shut-ins, soothing a grieving friend, answering a child's 482nd question when you feel that you have no more answers left.

This is all about relationship; a relationship of love and trust, first between you and your Good Shepherd, and then between you and your neighbor. In ancient cultures, predating David, the author of Psalm 23, it was quite common to compare kings and rulers to shepherds. In those times, a group's very existence depended solely on the ruler, just as the flock of sheep depended on their shepherd. In Psalm 23, David for the first time, shifts the comparison from the group to a personal relationship with God, our ruler.

> *"The Lord is MY Shepherd. I shall not want.*
> *He makes ME lie down in green pastures.*
> *He restores MY soul. Though I walk through*
> *the valley of the shadow of death, I will fear*
> *no evil. For you are with ME."*

We know love by this.

In his book *The Living Psalms*, Claus Westermann writes:

> *"The 23rd Psalm... is often viewed as a cheerful,*
> *ideal picture of a quite unreal relationship*
> *with God. That it is not, and that it never*
> *was... Above all, the intent of the text is not*
> *to paint a picture.... of either a shepherd or a*
> *lamb. What it does is to place two actions side*
> *by side: the provisions a shepherd makes for*
> *his flock and the provision God makes for the*
> *one who trusts in God. It is this trust... which,*
> *above all, makes it possible to compare God*

to a shepherd. But this trust rests in real-life
experience, in which suffering, anguish and
doubt all play a part. When a person, in all
that he experiences in life, seizes hold of trust -
whether worrying about daily bread or feeling
himself in deadly peril - when he trusts that
he will be upheld, that there is someone who
takes care of him, then, in and through that
trust, he has achieved fellowship with God
and he can say 'God is my shepherd'."

As with all good metaphors, the deeper you dig, the more trea-sures you find. Jesus/God as the shepherd and we as the sheep; we as the shepherds and our neighbors as the flock; we, ourselves called to serve a world that is difficult, sometimes unloveable, dirty, smelly, ornery, ungrateful, messy. We choose to do this because we have seen and experienced the Good Shepherd. We have been loved and we have value because of that love. We trust because we have seen trust. We voluntarily "lay down our life" for another.

Jesus said in the final verse of today's Gospel:

"No one takes my life from me, but I lay it down
of my own accord. I have the power to lay it
down and the power to take it up again. I have
received this command from my Father."

Mothers, Fathers, caring shepherds whose ministry we honor today, all God's people – we know love by this, that Jesus Christ laid down His life for us.

In some ways this church seems far away for St. John's in Leck Kill and that stained-glass window, far away in time and in dis-tance. And yet, they also seem one and the same, all part of God's grand design. The comforting arms of the Good Shepherd. The image grows and at the same time becomes even more personalized.

My prayer for us is that vision of the Good Shepherd, and the trusting relationship with the Good Shepherd, inspire us and challenge us to loving service every day.

8

The Inside of Your Hand

September 3, 2000
St. Michael Lutheran, Unionville, PA

SCRIPTURE READINGS: Deut. 4:1-9
Psalm 15
James 1:17-27
Mark 7:1-23

D o you remember from your school days, those students who dreaded and feared exams so much that they went to desperate measures in order to prepare. In an attempt to remember names, dates and formulas for the tests, they would write information on the bottom of their shoes, on their shirt lapels and even on their palms, the inside of their hands.

We all know that would be cheating. Right?

If, however, you wanted to put the best construction on their acts, you might say that they found the information so valuable, so precious, that they wanted to keep it as close to themselves as possible. This way they could have it ready for frequent reference, quick glances as reminder, so as not to forget any of it.

The ancient Israelites loved the Law. They believed that the Law was a divine gift from God. God had spoken to them personally from the mountain, through Moses, to give this gift. They memorized the words of the Law and taught it to their children. The Law represented a covenant with their God, but was also given as a guideline for living in community with others.

If you look at the most commonly known example of the Law – the 10 Commandments – you see that they really are about relationship. If you want to succeed at living in loving, healthy relationship with family and with community, you do not kill, you do not cheat, you do not commit adultery, you do not lie or steal.

God gave the gift of the Law because God desired a relationship with His people. And God desired that His people would have loving, healthy and happy relationships among themselves. The Law was a precious gift and the Israelites were adamant about keeping the words of the Law physically close to themselves, close to their thoughts and their hearts, so as not to forget a single detail.

Listen to this wonderful poetry by Huub Osterhuis, based on Deuteronomy 6:4:

> "Now into your care these words are given
> Cherish them, imprint them on your heart
> Make of them a weaving of your life
> Let you children learn as you repeat them
> Treasure them at home or far away
> As you lie down in sleep as well as when
>   you wake
> Take into your care these words that are
>   given to you.
> Hold them up, a sign of dedication
> Wrap them as a shawl about your head
> Hold them evermore before your eye
> Burn them on the framework of your door
> _Write them on the inside of your hand_

So will the length of your days, your time
of love increase,
And the years you share with sons
and daughters.
Your life will bloom and bear fruit like a
tree planted by a stream
Hear, O Israel."

Write them on the inside of your hand. Like the student, keeping his precious answers close to himself, so that they would not be forgotten, but even more profound.

The hand! Have you ever thought about all the things your hands do as you move through your day? They wash little faces; they clap with delight; they wave good-byes; they bring food to your mouth or, perhaps, the mouths of others; they type messages; they wipe a tear; the hands turn the pages of a book; they embrace someone dear.

Hands! If, as the poet Osterhuis says, you write the words of God's Law on the inside of your hand, with each of the tasks we mentioned, God's beloved Law for healthy living and loving, is right there for you to see each time those hands open, or pass close to the heart.

All of today's readings have to do with laws for living happily in relationship. Look at the words of Psalm 15:

"Lord, who can dwell with you? He who leads a
blameless life, speaks truth from the heart, does
no evil to his friends, does not heap contempt
upon his neighbor."

Those few sentences tell us not only how to dwell with our God, but how to live happily with each other.

In the passage from the book of James, we read this:

"...let everyone be quick to listen, slow to speak, slow to anger, be doers, not merely hearers which deceive themselves."

As with all good things, there is definitely a flip side to the goodness of the Law. There can be abuse of its original intent. It is one thing to love God's Law, and quite another to become enslaved by the human traditions that build up around keeping the Law, traditions that alienate, destroy and harm others or adversely affect relationships.

There is an interesting story which illustrates this all too well: One day a young girl was watching her mother preparing a roast for the evening meal. Just before placing it into the roasting pan, her mother lopped off a bit from each end of the roast, and then put all of the meat in the pan and popped it into the oven. When the girl questioned her mother as to why she cut the ends off, her mother replied, "That's the way it's done." No amount of inquiry resulted in an answer as to WHY it was done that way, just that grandmother did it that way, too. So, the young girl asked further and was finally able to ascertain that long ago, the very first roast and been too large for the very first roasting pan, and so the ends were cut off to make it fit. The tradition stuck. No one thought to question it. Today, it might no longer be necessary, but the tradition in this family had become law, just by having been repeated for generations.

I doubt very much whether the chopping off of the ends of a roast adversely affected any relationships in this story, but it does illustrate how the original intent got lost in tradition. The family had become trapped by the LETTER of the law and had forgotten the SPIRIT of the law.

In today's Gospel from St. Mark, the scribes and Pharisees noticed that some of Jesus' disciples "were eating with defiled hands," that is, without having washed their hands. So, the scribes and Pharisees asked Jesus, "Why do your disciples eat with defiled hands?"

Hands again? We talked earlier about keeping the Law close by writing on the inside of the hand. Now, again with the hands, defiled because they had not been washed. We're not talking about any ordinary hand-washing here. We're looking at serious ritual washing required by the strictest Orthodox Jews, for themselves and for all around them who claimed to be religious. Edershem, in his book *The Life And Times Of Jesus The Messiah*, outlines the most elaborate of these ritual washings.

> "Water jars were kept at the ready to be used before a meal. The minimum amount of water to be used was a quarter of a log, which is defined as enough water to fill one and a half egg shells. The water was first poured on both hands, held with the fingers pointed upward, and must run up the arm as far as the wrist. It must drop off from the wrist, for the water itself is now unclean, having touched the unclean hands; and if it ran down the fingers again, it would render them unclean. The process was repeated with the hands held in the opposite direction, with the fingers pointed down; and then finally, each hand was cleansed by being rubbed with the fist of the other. A really strict Jew would do all this, not only before a meal, but also between each of the courses."

To the Orthodox Jew, all of this ritual ceremony was religion; this is what, as they believed, God demanded of them. Religion had become identified with a host of external regulations. It had become as important to do ritual hand-washing as it was to obey the commandments:

"Thou shalt not kill"

and

"Thou shalt not steal."

Jesus answered the scribes and Pharisees with an accusation:

"You abandon the commandment of God and hold to human tradition. Listen to me all of you, and understand; there is nothing outside a person that by going in can defile it, but the things that come out are what defile it. For it is within the human heart that evil intentions come."

To the scribes and Pharisees, worship WAS ritual, ceremony, all done according to their Law. To Jesus, worship was the clean heart and the loving life. William Temple, Archbishop of Canterbury (1942-44), once said:

"To worship is to quicken the conscience by the holiness of God, to fill the mind with the truth of God, to purge the imagination by the beauty of God, to open the heart to the love of God and to devote the will to the purpose of God."

We might want to read those words at least once a day.

According to a certain story, Queen Victoria was once at a diplomatic reception in London. The guest of honor was an African chieftain. All went well during the meal itself, until, at the end, finger bowls were served. The guest of honor had never seen a British finger bowl, and no one had thought to brief him beforehand about its purpose. So, he took the finger bowl in his hands, lifted it to his mouth, and drank its contents, down to the last drop.

For an instant, there was breathless silence among the British upper crust, and then they began to whisper to one another.

All that stopped in the next instant as the Queen silently took her finger bowl in her hands, lifted it to her lips, and drank its contents, down to the last drop. A moment later, 500 surprised British ladies and gentlemen simultaneously drank the contents of their finger bowls.

It was against the rules of English etiquette to drink from the finger bowl, but on that particular evening, Victoria set aside those rules in order to preserve a relationship. She was, after all, the Queen.

This story is a wonderful illustration of how NOT to use the Law, or human traditions, to hurt, alienate, destroy or pass judgement; but how to use actions, behaviors, deeds and judgements to love, to welcome, to include and accept, to build up and affirm others.

We must be careful to come away from this message with the correct understanding. I remind myself, "Don't go to Mark without taking Deuteronomy along." Too often we think Old Testament = LAW, who needs it; New Testament = Gospel, very good. We need both Law and Gospel, otherwise we might not only teach disparaging things about another culture's traditions, but that, in so doing, we distance ourselves from Jesus' words, believing they certainly do not apply to us. We forget to look inside ourselves to see what is coming out that is defiling ourselves and others.

The Deuteronomy text affirms the life-giving goodness of the Law, as long as the spirit and the heart of the Law don't get lost in human tradition. The heart and spirit of the Law are in the great commandment from Deuteronomy 6:

> "You shall love the Lord your God with all your heart, and with all your soul and with all your mind."

When you know this, you will live your life in response to the divine gift of the Law.

Remember these words:

"Wrap them as a shawl about your head
Hold them evermore before your eyes
Burn them on the framework of your door
Write them on the inside of your hand
So will the length of your days, your time of
*   life increase*
And the years you spend with your sons
*   and daughters.*
Your life will bloom and bear fruit like a
*   tree planted by a stream.*
Hear, O Israel."

9

Take Off the Graveclothes

November 5, 2000
St. Michael Lutheran, Unionville, PA

(This message was offered prior to the performance of *Requiem*
by Gabriel Faure.)

Scripture Readings: Isaiah 25:69
                                    John 11:21-23, 38-443

A
Requiem Mass is traditionally sung at the time of a death.
Still today, in our Roman churches, this is the custom.

On All Saints Sunday we celebrate with joy, and with songs
of praise, but also with prayer and quiet devotion, the lives of the
saints who have gone before us, those whom we love who have died
and been resurrected. So, it is fitting, on this day, All Saints Sunday,
to sing a Requiem. Yes, a Requiem is a mass for the dead, but more
accurately, a Requiem is a mass for the resurrected. We live in the
hope and the promise given to us by the life and death and resurrection of Jesus Christ. So, death for us is not an end, but a threshold
into a new life. We live in the promise of that resurrection.

In the Requiem, we are praying in and for that promise.

The first words in this Requiem are:

> "Rest eternal grant them, Lord our God we pray
> to you."

And then:

> "Free them from utter darkness, grant them
> deliverance."

Following that, we sing:

> "Deliver me Lord.....trembling I stand before you."

At the outset, the sung text is meant for all who have died, but subtly, in the preceding example, the prayer has turned personal, a prayer of concern for ourselves, for us the living.

In the last movement, *In Paradisium*, we sing:

> "God's angels lead you into Paradise. Choirs of
> angels sing you to your rest, and with Lazarus,
> may you be raised to eternal life."

What wonderful imagery here, not only to be LED into Paradise by the angels, but to SUNG into Paradise by those angels. We WILL rise again!

Jesus went to the tomb of Lazarus, in today's Gospel reading from John. Lazarus had already died and had been buried 4 days earlier. Crowds followed Jesus, as they always did. At the mouth of the tomb, Jesus cried out in a loud voice:

> "Lazarus, come out!"

The dead man came out, his hands and feet bound with strips of cloth and his face wrapped in cloth. This was the custom in those days, to wrap the body in a shroud. This shroud was also known as the graveclothes.

Then Jesus said to those who had come to the tomb with Him:

> "Unbind him and let him go."

In other words, "Take off the graveclothes and let him go free."

There are three actions that Jesus commands:

Come out of the tomb.

Take off the graveclothes.

Go free.

This scene points to our being raised, after death, to a new life. Jesus is demonstrating to us that, like Lazarus, we will rise again.

Even more significantly, this story is meant for the living saints, for all of us. I would ask you, what are the graveclothes that are binding you, and preventing you from living freely and unrestrained in the hope and promise of God's love? Are you bound by the graveclothes of despair? Of depression? Are you bound by the graveclothes of fear? Of addiction? Are you bound by the graveclothes of anger? Of greed? Are you shrouded in hate, envy and deceit?

Take off those graveclothes. God has made you a promise. God says:

"You will rise again and live with me. Here in life, I am always with you. And I will not remember any of your sins."

Mary and Martha said to Jesus:

"If you had been here, my brother would not have died,"

Jesus answers:

"I am here, Come out of the tomb. Take off those graveclothes. Go free."

10

Story of a Lifetime

November 30, 2010
Heartland Hospice Memorial Service

NOTE: I was asked not to make this message too "Christian," since our assembly was comprised of people of all faiths and perhaps those with no belief system at all.

TELL YOUR STORIES

"Tell me a story." Any of you who are parents, grandparents, aunts, uncles, caretakers, have heard that phrase. Often when we would get that request as young parents, we would tell our children the story of Georg (Gay-org). You might recognize Georg as the European pronunciation of the familiar name George.

"Once upon a time.." we would begin, "there was a young boy about your age, 4 years old, who lived in Germany, all the way across the huge Atlantic Ocean. His family decided that they would seek a new life in America. So they boarded a big ship and set off for the new country across the ocean. At times the sea was very rough and the ship would creak and groan as it tusseled with the enormous waves. Georg would shiver with fright, huddling up close to his parents for comfort and safety.."

"Presently Georg's family arrived in the new country – America, docking in the harbor at the city of Baltimore. They looked for a place to live and for jobs so that they could earn a living. Their first jobs were as farm laborers. Even though Georg was very little, he helped out whenever he could."

"Georg grew up, married and had a family of his own. One of his sons was named John. When John grew up and married, he had two daughters – Evelyn and Miriam. Miriam became your grand-mother."

Did my children ever meet Georg? Did they ever know his family? No. He lived many, many years ago, before they were born. He was their great, great grandfather. But because we told them Georg's story, the story of his lifetime, he was very much alive in their hearts. To them he became a real-life character, connected to them, establishing for them their place in the larger story.

That is the reason we are here tonight, to tell the story of a life-time. I can't do it for you because the stories are yours. YOU need to tell them. We are all gathered here for the same reason – we have lost someone who was very dear to us. How is it that we can honor them, keep them alive in our hearts and in the hearts of those who love us?

Tell stories.

At first the telling is difficult. Perhaps what we focus on is their last few days, the surroundings, the good-byes, the tender caretak-ing. But as we journey through the pain and the grief, we will find ourselves able to recall other aspects of that person's life that we want to tell. Maybe it is not an event or deed at first, but perhaps the special twinkle in their eyes, the telltale twitch of humor on a mischievous face. And suddenly the recollections will make you think of a story.

TELL it!

For me, it was the way my Mother's eyes looked when she smiled. Hers wasn't just a smile of the lips but of the entire face. And then I go on to think of an occasion where that smile lingered for SO long. And here it comes!!! A story!!!! Mother called me one day from home, a farm about 120 miles north of here, the farm on which I grew up. She asked, "Joanne, could you take me shopping for a new dress for Natalie's wedding?" I agreed, but had some doubts about how this would work out, since Mother, by this time, was having a lot of difficulty moving around. I couldn't imagine trudging through the mall with her, and I knew she had too much pride to be pushed in a wheelchair.

So, I came up with a plan. Here at home, I dashed out to Sears and Penney's, Mother's two favorite stores. I bought seven dresses that I thought she might like, piled them into my car, and made the 2 and ½ hour drive to Leck Kill. I walked into the house, laden with an armful of dresses, and announced "We're going to have a fashion show!"

Remember that smile I described? There it was, and it crept onto her face slowly as she realized what I meant.

We had quite a time that day. Mother would put on a dress in the living room and then enter the kitchen to model it for Dad, who dutifully sat and watched. His eyes had that special twinkle as he smiled, enjoying Mother's sheer delight. She was like a young girl again! We had such fun!

After all 7 dresses had been modeled, we were faced with a dilemma! Mother liked two dresses equally well and couldn't make a choice. So Dad – usually a very frugal man- pulled out his checkbook, and with a very uncharacteristic gesture said, "Let's take both" as he wrote out a check for not one, but two dresses.

Have you ever met my parents? Were they acquaintances of yours? Not likely. Do you feel as if you know them now? I think so. This is the value of telling your stories. Keep those you love alive in your hearts AND introduce them to us, the ones who love and support you.

LISTEN TO STORIES

That brings me to the second part of my message. This part involves all of you, the family and friends, those who support the ones who grieve. If it is their task to TELL the stories, it is our task to LISTEN to those stories. The best support you can give is to listen.

Not distracted listening, where you are doing something else and half hear. I mean the kind of listening where you sit still, establish eye contact, nod, understanding that this is the best gift you can give – to just BE there and listen, and really hear what is being said.

In the Beatitudes we hear these words:

> *"Blessed are those who mourn, for they shall be comforted."*

That's us, the comforters! How do we comfort? We listen and then listen some more, even if we've heard the stories again and again.

For a time I volunteered as a driver to take Senior citizens from their Luther Towers residence to medical appointments. On those excursions, I had a lot of opportunity to listen. Every person had a story and I was most eager to hear it. Most stories revolved around a life mate who had died, some recently and others many years ago. "He was the love of my life," one petite little lady told me one day. "Every day he would leave me a love note when he left for work, and every Friday he would bring me flowers. He never missed, never forgot." I had never met her man, but all of a sudden, I was bound up in their love story, their story of a lifetime. I felt as if I knew her husband. I liked him! He came to life for me, just as he was alive in her heart.

LIVE IN HOPE

If your job is telling the stories and your comforter's job is listening to those stories, then what is it that I can do? I see my job as bringing you the message of Hope and Promise.

If we begin our story with "Once upon a time..." then what do we say at the conclusion? "They lived happily ever after. THE END." Right? THE END! I'm here to tell you, I don't think so! I don't think this is the end of the story. I would rather say "The story of a lifetime, the continuing saga."

Every culture has had its beliefs about what comes after death, the afterlife, whether it's the Egyptians and their pyramids or the

Chinese and their Terra Cotta Warriors.

A Native-American poem reads this way:

> "Don't stand by my grave and weep, for I am not
> there. I do not sleep. I am a thousand winds that
> blow. I am the diamond's glint on snow. I am
> the sunlight on ripened grain. I am the gentle
> autumn's rain. Don't stand by my grave and
> cry. I am not there. I did not die."

In more modern philosophy: God created the dimension of time. When you die, you simply exit the dimension of time.

You see, we don't really KNOW in here (indicate head/brain) what comes next, but we DO know in here (indicate heart). Our story will not be "THE END!" What I am calling you to do is to live in the Hope and the Promise. Your story IS a continuing saga!!!

FROM THE BIBLE

John 14:

> "I go before you to prepare a place for you.
> Would I tell you this if it were not so?"

Rev 21:

> "He will wipe away every tear from your eyes
> and death shall be no more, neither shall there
> be mourning or crying or pain"

Ps 91:

> "And He will raise you up on eagles' wings,
> bear you on the breath of dawn, make you to
> shine like the sun, and hold you in the palm of
> His hands."

Is 43:

> *"I have called you by name; you are mine.*
> *When you pass through the water I will be*
> *with you and through the rivers, they shall not*
> *overwhelm you; when you walk through the*
> *fire you shall not be burned and the flame shall*
> *not consume you.*

Matt:

> *"Come to me all you who are weary and heavy*
> *laden and I will give you rest."*

John:

> *"Peace I leave with you, my peace I give you.*
> *I will not leave you comfortless."*

TELL YOUR STORY OF A LIFETIME.

LISTEN TO THE STORIES OF OTHERS.

LIVE IN HOPE AND PROMISE.

11

The Prodigal

October 13, 2010
First Presbyterian, Newark DE
SCRIPTURE READINGS: Luke 15:11-323

Dedicated to Carl Nelson

O Love that will not let me go
I rest my weary soul on thee
I give thee back the life I owe...

Once upon a time in a land far, far away, there was a family - a father and two sons. The youngest son took all his inheritance, left home, spent it all and then returned home. The father took him back. The older son was mad. And they lived happily ever after. The end.

Not much of a story when told that way, is it? We have to acknowledge that Jesus was quite the storyteller. Every tale had a point, or many points and had characters in them that were meant to show us ourselves and our errant ways. Storytelling was Jesus' favorite teaching tool. I find it fascinating that even today, over 2000 years later we are still reading these stories, these parables, analyzing them, and finding important meanings that apply to our lives.

You've heard the parable of the Prodigal many times, probably more than other parables. Then, why ever would I choose it for my message today? Been there, done that you might mutter as you settle down for a nap.

Stay with me and let's see if we can discover some new elements that we hadn't ever considered before. As I did the exegesis on this passage, I found it to be more and more compelling.

When I told a friend that I would be preaching on the parable of the Prodigal Son, he raised the question "Who is the most stressed out character in this story?" I thought the son, the father and the older brother were in different ways equally stressed. But I was wrong. My friend told me that the most stressed character was the fatted calf!.

I'll bet that one was new to you. See, we're already on a roll.

Did you know that Jesus never used the word Prodigal? Some translator or editor along the way chose this name for the younger son and it definitely stuck. The word actually is found in vs. 13, where the term Jesus used is "waster."

Prodigal is an interesting word. In addition to the meaning we associate with it, i.e. one who is wasteful, it can also mean "bountiful, lavish or profuse." Discovering that truth, I had to reconsider my judgmental attitude toward the younger son. Perhaps his wastefulness was rooted in a kind of generosity toward those whom he met and with whom he associated. Wastefulness as generosity! We can probably identify with that. Sometimes others see the causes we support and to which we make donations as a waste of time and resources.

THE SETTING

Where exactly was Jesus' storytelling taking place? In Luke, Chapter 14, where this series of parables began, it reads:

> "One Sabbath, when Jesus went to eat at the
> house of a prominent Pharisee, He was being
> carefully watched."

A prominent Pharisee. Jesus was being carefully watched.

Who were these Pharisees? They were one of the three major religious societies of Judaism at the time of the New Testament. The Pharisees were the most vocal, powerful and influential.

The Hebrew name Pharisee means separatists or the separated ones. The Pharisees meant to obey God's commands, but eventually they became so devoted and extremist in very limited parts of the Law, that they were blind to the Messiah when He stood in their very midst. They saw His miracles and heard His words, but instead of believing with joy, they sought to stop Him. They saw Jesus as a threat to their position and power. Sound familiar?

THE AUDIENCE

Who was in the audience for Jesus' teaching and storytelling? Three groups, as I see it:

1) The Pharisees, of course, in whose home Jesus was dining.

2) "Tax collectors and sinners" Luke says in Chapter 15, vs. 1.

> *"Now the tax collectors and sinners were gathering around to hear Him. But the Pharisees and teachers of the Law muttered 'This man welcomes sinners and eats with them.' "*

The use of the word sinners in this quote from the Pharisees is a pretty good indicator of their attitude. There's us, the good and sinless and then there's everyone else, the sinners.

3) We are in the audience. Thousands of years after the telling, we read and reread the parable, struggling to understand more completely, placing ourselves into the story, identifying with the characters.

THE CHARACTERS

Where do you see yourself in the story?

This parable is not an allegory like some of the others, but a story drawn from real life. The younger son asks for his inheritance right now, which was a perfectly legal thing to do. He leaves home and squanders that fortune on "wild living," according to vs. 13.

Is this you? Have you ever squandered the love and trust of faithful friends? Have you squandered and wasted the beautiful, natural gifts of the Earth? Have you taken for granted the amazing grace of our God and lived as if you have no need to acknowledge that God?

Preceding this particular parable, there are two other stories concerning things that were lost – the lost coin and the lost sheep. The poor woman who lost the coin and the shepherd who lost the sheep would not rest until what was lost was found.

Joachim Jeremias in his book *The Parables of Jesus* says this:

> *"To call a man lost is to pay him a high*
> *compliment, for it means that he is precious*
> *in the sight of God."*

The theme of all three parables is that something precious is lost and then found.

The one difference in the story of the prodigal is that it contains and element not found in the other two. That element is repentance. Vs. 17 reads:

> *"When he came to his senses, he decided to*
> *return home and say to his father, 'I have sinned*
> *against heaven and earth and against you. I am*
> *no longer worthy to be called your son. Make*
> *me like one of your hired men.'"*

In the former parables, the sheep and the coin did not repent.

Jesus' point in including the element of repentance is that our loving God will forgive anything, as long as we recognize the sin and are truly sorry, and intent on changing our ways.

I saw one of those outdoor church signs the other day which read: "You might be outside the Will of God, but never outside the

Reach of God."

So, the younger son returns home, receives not only forgiveness, but gifts – a robe, the sign of royalty, a ring, the symbol of authority and shoes, a sign of wealth. Only slaves and hired servants went without shoes. And, he was treated as an honored guest, complete with a feast featuring a fatted calf. There was genuine rejoicing because what was lost, what was most precious, was now found.

That brings us to our next character. Guess who was not happy with the feasting and rejoicing. The older son!

Vs. 28 reads:

> "The older son became angry and refused to
> go in. So, his father went out and pleaded
> with him."

We can picture it, can't we? The defiance, the arms crossed over the chest, the scowl and the hostile retort, "It's just not fair."

Is this you? Have you ever said "After all I've done for you!!!" Have you held onto a grudge? Have you considered yourself a faithful follower of God, but expect to be recognized and rewarded for it?

What's interesting about Jesus' account of the older son is that he simply lets the story hang there. He doesn't say anything more about the older son. Did he join the banquet? Did he repent? Did he stay angry and hostile? Did he leave home?

For those of us who like things to end up neat and tidy, this is disquieting. What happened? Isn't there a sequel?

Actually, this lack of conclusion was deliberate on Jesus' part. You see, he was preaching to those pesky Pharisees, and to us, using the older son as a metaphor. Jeremias writes:

> "He still has hope of moving them to abandon
> their resistance to the Gospel. He still hopes that
> they will recognize how their self-righteousness
> and lovelessness separates them from God and

that they may come to experience the great joy
which the Good News brings."

Finally, we consider the character of the father.

Some people suggest that this parable be called The Compassionate Father, that it's really about him and not the wasteful son.

"O Love that will not let me go
I rest my weary soul on thee
I give thee back the life I owe"

The text of this old favorite hymn and the compassionate father are, for me, inseparable. The father honors his son's selfish wishes. The father continues to love him and to watch for his return. When he sees his son in the distance, the father runs to him. He doesn't just stand there expecting the son to come to him. He runs to meet him. He gives him gifts and a banquet. We love this father. We love this man. We want to know him. His love would not let that son go.

I attended the theater in NYC a few years ago to see Prokofiev's ballet *The Prodigal Son*. The finale showed the father standing regally with a crown, a jeweled robe and a gold staff. The son, in rags, lying on his belly, dragged himself slowly and painfully across the stage. With great drama, the father carefully opened his generous robe, gently enclosing the son in its depths. The son was no longer visible, as if he and the father were now one. So stunning was this amazing conclusion that the theater remained totally silent for several moments as the audience struggled to come up with the appropriate response. Then, as one body, we came to our feet in thunderous applause.

The compassionate father welcomed the son home exactly as we would want to be welcomed – God embracing us into the generous folds of His robe. We would become one with Him. We love this compassionate God. We want to know Him.

O love that will not let me go

The writer Henri Nowen says:

"Here is a God I want to believe in, a father who from the dawn of creation has stretched out His arms in merciful blessing, never forcing Himself on anyone, but always waiting, never letting His arms drop down in despair, but always hoping His children will return so that He can speak words of love to them and put His tired arms upon their shoulders."

"O Love that will not let me go
I rest my weary soul on thee
I give thee back the life I owe

O Joy that seeks me through pain
I cannot close my heart to thee
I trace the rainbow through the rain
And feel the promise is not vain
That morn shall tearless be"

12

Theology That Sings

June 10, 2018
First Presbyterian Church, Newark DE

C hoir had just sung:

"O Jeremiah, Open up the Book"
O Jeremiah, open up the book
Shine a little glory in the dark of night
O Jeremiah, open up the book
Open our eyes. Open our hearts.

O Jeremiah, open up the book. The book. The Holy Bible! Read it. It's all there, all those wonderful stories – Abraham, Sarah, Moses, Aaron, Miriam, Jacob, Elijah, Mary. Jesus!!!! Open the book. It's all in there.

I grew up in a small farming village where the church was the center, not only of our spiritual life, but social life, too. My parents were active teachers, Council members, choir singers. All of us cared for the building, cleaning, painting, maintaining... I never heard of a sexton till I moved to the city. There was always a lot of Bible reading going on – Grandmas with the Bible open right next to their favorite chair, devotions at the supper table before you started eating......

My sister and I shared a bedroom and every night we would read aloud a chapter from the Bible. It took us over three years. I think we did it at least twice. But still, I felt guilt. I wasn't reading the Bible enough. How many of you read the Bible enough? Raise your hands. You know that guilt that is implanted at an early age with expectations that we never quite can live up to.

My passion was music, always singing, playing piano at age 5, organ at 12 even though I had difficulty reaching the foot pedals. I was accompanying congregational singing at age 9. Passion!!! I couldn't get enough of it. I remember distinctly the first time I sang a harmony part. The sound was glorious. I was sure the heavens had opened up and God would descend any moment. Passion!!!

So, this guilt (Joanne, you're not reading the Bible enough) and this passion for music existed side by side for a long time. Until gradually I started to realize that my faith, my theology was taking shape because of the music. Bishop Anselm, a 12th Century bishop of Canterbury, said:

"Theology is faith seeking understanding."

I was seeking and gaining understanding of my faith through the music. God works in wondrous ways!!! I realized that it was in the depths of music that I most often was able to encounter the transcendent God.

Let me illustrate. Could you quote for me Job, Chapter 19? Have you ever read it? Maybe? Not sure? However, if I said:

"I know that my redeemer liveth"

I bet for sure that you would be hearing that beautiful solo from Handel's *Messiah*. That text comes directly from the book of Job, Chapter 19.

If I asked you to recite something from Matthew, Chapter 11, could you do it? But if I sang:

"Come unto me all ye that labor"

I am sure your ears would ring with that beautiful solo again from *Messiah.* There it is, right out of Matthew, Chapter 11.

Or how about Psalm 84? Hmm! How does that go? But, if I said:

"How lovely is thy dwelling place."

Again the tune takes over and, once again, the Word lives through that beautiful chorus from Brahms' *Requiem.*

So, we are fortunate that we have Theology that Sings. If our theology is faith seeking understanding, then as we sing or listen to music, our faith is coming alive. We are getting glimpses of the transcendent God. Our theology is being formed.

We call this Spirit of Music Sunday. On this day we feature all of the wonderful musicians and music teams with which we are blessed here at First Pres. Let's explore that title for just a moment. Take the word SPIRIT. This is inherited from the Latin, of course, as so many of our words are. Consider for a moment that the word for spirit and the word for air or breath in Latin are the same. Spirit. Respiration – our very act of breathing in air. We take in air and at the same time take in the SPIRIT. Inspire – breathe in the spirit and be creative; conceive a new idea. Aspire – breathe in the SPIRIT and be strengthened to achieve a higher goal. SPIRIT, air, breath. Think how fortunate we are, gathered here. Together, we breathe in air, we breathe in the SPIRIT, and then out of that SPIRIT/air comes our song. We breathe in the Spirit/air and from our mouths come the words:

"Our Father, who art in heaven..."

We breathe in the Spirit/air and together we say:

"I believe...;"

Infused with this Spirit/air, together we sing our faith, our theology. How wonderful is that?

About a decade ago the group Pearl Jam put out a song called

Breathe, Just Breathe. One verse goes like this:

> *"Chaos calls but all you really need*
> *Is to take it in, fill your lungs.*
> *The peace of God that overcomes*
> *Breathe, just breathe*
> *Come and rest at my feet*
> *And be, just be*
> *Chaos calls but all you really need*
> *Is to breathe, just breathe."*

Pearl Jam got it right, didn't they?

> *"Breathe on me breath of God, so that I never*
> *die. So that I love as Thou dost love and do*
> *what Thou wouldst do."*

Now, think back to Genesis, the very first book in the Bible. (O Jeremiah, open up the Book). God is kneeling in the mud and the dirt. God has just formed a being out of mud and clay and dust and then :

> *"God breathed into his nostrils the breath of life.*
> *And man became a living thing."*

Man became a living thing!! WOW! That is beautiful and powerful stuff!

Finally, let's talk about hymns. I love to say "Hymns have faith value."

How, for example, can you sing the beautiful *O Love That Will Not Let Me Go* and NOT think of the prodigal son? We are that prodigal trying to come home. God, like the father in the story, doesn't just wait at the door. God runs to greet us and welcome us home.

Or the hymn, *Love Divine All Loves Excelling*, final stanza:

> *"Finish then thy new creation,*

pure and spotless let us be....
Till we cast our crowns before Thee,
lost in wonder, love and praise."

Or how can we sing that old favorite *I Come to the Garden Alone* and not see Mary, who has come to the tomb to anoint the body, and instead, encounters the risen Lord, face to face, in the garden on that first Easter morning.

How blessed are we? We breathe in the SPIRIT, that divine breath, and out of our mouths, together, we sing our faith. How blessed are we? We have a theology that sings.

Amen.

13

Wonderfully Made

October 14, 2018
First Presbyterian Church, Newark DE
SCRIPTURE READINGS: Psalm 139

Not long ago as I was doing the organ substitute circuit, I found myself in a small Episcopal church in Newport. Let me set up the scene for you – beautiful small church. Congregation numbered about 30 people, we had done some hymns, knelt to confess our sins, and heard the reading of the scriptures. Now it was time for the sermon, at which point the priest got up and introduced 10-year-old Sarah.

Sarah stood tall, and with a strong, confident voice read this book to the congregation.

(Read *Runaway Bunny*)

When she had finished there was total silence. She quietly returned to her seat. The priest wisely said no more.

I could hardly sit still on the organ bench. I looked around to see if anyone else had heard what I heard. The moment was so profound. Had anyone else heard in the reading of that children's book the whole of Psalm 139?

"Where can I flee from your presence?"

says the Psalmist.

"I am running away,"

says the little bunny.

From Ps. 139:

"If I go to the heavens, you are there."

From The Runaway Bunny:

"I will be a bird and fly away from you."

*"If I rise on the wings of the dawn,
if I settle on the far side of the sea,"*

says the Psalmist.

*"I will become a sailboat and sail away
from you,"*

says the Runaway Bunny.

In each and every case, the mother bunny had an answer: I will always be with you. I will bring you home. In every case God has the answer for us: I will be with you everywhere you go.

For me the voice of God, the Word of God, had literally leaped from the pages of that book and the mouth of that sweet young girl. I was profoundly moved.

Later, I was sharing this experience with one of my friends and she said, "You know, my daughter hates that psalm. It makes her feel as if God is always spying on her, judging everything she does."

I see it differently. I chose to see God with me in everything I do, in every place that I go.

Here's an example: My family was vacationing at the beach. On a beautiful, sunny day, some of the adults were snoozing or reading while basking in the abundant sunshine. My daughter and two sons-in-law were diving into the waves some distance from the sand. My granddaughter, about 3 years old, was playing happily at the edge of the water. Suddenly, to my horror, a rogue wave developed and began moving toward the water's edge. Before we adults could struggle out of our beach chairs and run to help, the wave was breaking, and, we imagined doing its worst. However, I looked out to see three arms extended above the deep, deep water, the arms of my daughter and two sons-in-law. Cradled in those hands was Hannah being held in safety high above the water. What was Hannah doing? She was giggling! She had no idea that she was in any kind of danger.

What better place to be than right in the palm of God's hands, unaware that we have anything to fear. Giggle a little! God is with us. Giggle a little. Enjoy the freedom from fear, knowing God offers us protection.

Let's talk about fear.

I have a fear of flying. I fly because I have places to go and things to see. You can talk to me all day long about aerodynamics and I still say that unwieldy behemoth should not be able to hang up there in the sky with me and 100 other people in it!!!! Perhaps I don't trust anything that I'm not driving.

So I have my mantras:

Isaiah 43:1:

> *"Do not be afraid, I am with you. I have called you each by name."*

OR Psalm 91 –

> *"He will raise you up on eagles' wings. You need not fear the terrors of the night or the arrows that fly by day. I will protect you because you call my name."*

OR Isaiah 12:2

> *"Surely it is God who saves me. I will trust in God and not be afraid. For God is my rock and my sure defense and He will be my Savior."*

Did you know that the words "Fear not" or "Don't be afraid" appear 360 times in the Bible? Pretty strong message, isn't it. Fear not for I am with you – even better.

The prophet Micah says:

> *"Walk humbly with God."*

Scholars say that Micah, using the word HUMBLY, was trying to establish the difference between the long, fast, stride of the powerful and rich, with the calm assurance one experiences when walking with God.

It's a partnership, you and God. Think of Jesus words in Matt. 11:28:

> *"Come to me all you who are weary and heavy-laden and I will give you rest. For my yoke is easy and my burden is light."*

Jesus doesn't mean to tie you down with a heavy yoke around your neck. Jesus is illustrating the partnership between you and your God. A yoke is not fitted on just one ox or beast of burden but is meant for two. A team; a partnership.

You know that I come from a farming background. By the time I came along, we had tractors. We were no longer farming with teams of oxen or mules. But often these relics from the past, these antiques, like yokes for a team, would be hanging on barn walls. Words of wisdom from an old farmer – "a yoke is meant for a team to work together, pulling the plow or the harvester. But did you know that one of the team was always the stronger, the more experienced, the leader? And his team mate knew to follow and trust his leadership."

Remember earlier when I said I see God in everything? What a moment! God in the barn, for Pete's sake, speaking through an old farmer.

PARTNERSHIP

In one of my morning meditations I came across this statement: "Prayer puts us in partnership with God." Prayer puts us in partnership with God. Haven't you ever wondered why you pray? What good does it do? We can't tell God WHAT to do or WHEN to do what we think is needed. Yes, prayer changes the Pray-er. But when you think of prayer putting you in partnership with God, it takes on a whole new meaning. Together you and God are working it out. Together you and God are speaking the name of someone you love. Together with God, you pray more consciously for the good of ALL, not just self. And furthermore, if all God's people are praying in partnership with God, think how closely that unites us.

God is with you in partnership. God dwells in you, as you. You are wonderfully made – in God's image, no less. What a tremendous gift and what an awesome responsibility.

Psalms 139:7-10:

> "Where can I go from your Spirit? Where can I flee from your presence? If I go to the heavens, you are there. If I make my bed in the depths, you are there. If I rise up on the wings of the dawn, if I settle on the far side of the sea, even there your hand will guide me, you right hand will hold me fast. I praise you because I am fearfully and wonderfully made."

Fear not, I am with you. I have called you each by name.

He will raise you up on eagle's wings. You shall not fear the terrors of the night

Do justice, love mercy and walk humbly with God.

You know what? There's some good stuff in here (lift Bible), and it comes to us sometimes in and from unexpected places. God created us in God's own image. We are wonderfully made. We walk humbly with God and through prayer are privileged to be in partnership with God.

Amen.

14

Seek Ye First

March 24, 2019

First Presbyterian Church, Newark DE

SCRIPTURE READINGS: John 6:56-71
                    Matthew 5:1-13

INTRODUCTION

Newspapers (To begin, I held up recent newspapers and read a few headlines. I followed each headline with these words: "Lord to whom shall we go? You have the words of eternal life").

In our first reading today, Jn.6:53, Jesus is on a hillside with a crowd of people listening to Him preach. He has just fed the 5000. He says:

> *"I am the bread of life. Unless you eat my flesh and drink my blood... you will have no life in you."*

People begin to leave, not understanding what sounds to them like very gruesome talk. The only ones left are His 12 disciples
Peter says:

> *"Lord, this is difficult to hear. How can we accept this?"*

Jesus responds to His disciples

"Are you leaving too?"

And they answer:

"Lord to whom shall we go? You have the words of eternal life."

Lord to whom shall WE go? You have the words of eternal life.

In our second reading, from Matthew's account of the Sermon on the Mount, Jesus is on another hillside, again preaching to the multitudes who gather.

Jesus has the words:

"Don't worry about what you should eat or drink or wear. Seek Ye first the kingdom of God and His righteousness, and all these things shall be added unto you.

And again:

"Seek ye first the kingdom of God and His righteousness, and all these things shall be added unto you."

Now there is a sentence worthy of consideration. It is loaded. Let's have a closer look.

KINGDOM OF GOD

First off, I bristle at the word kingdom. It hints at a hierarchy, where there is someone higher than the everyone else, one who reaps the benefits from overworking or overtaxing his underlings; one who is wealthy and grants special favors when it suits his needs; one who can dispose of one of his subjects, just because he has been offended; one who owns all the land (or thinks he should) and gives it away to reap more rewards from its natural resources.

It's easy to understand why Jesus used the term kingdom when preaching on the mount. In his day, Kingdoms were everywhere. Your power was determined by how many kingdoms you could conquer or overthrow. The Hebrew nation begged God for a king until God finally granted them Saul and then the great King David. The Jews waited for a King as the Messiah, the anointed one and were disappointed that Jesus was NOT the conquering hero they had imagined.

Our founding Fathers worked very hard to free us from any kind of kingship. George Washington refused to be named a king. We have been raised to think instead of "We the people..." We do not have a king forced on us by family succession, but a leader by vote of we the people.

In my research, however, I found the term Kingdom of God defined as "wherever God reigns." *Wherever God reigns.* OK. That's better. But truthfully, that definition quickly leads to more questions.

What does that mean "Wherever God reigns?" Does God reign here and now OR is this a place in the future, a heaven that we look forward to? Is it now or simply in the future?

Jesus said in Luke 17:21:

> *"The Kingdom of God is in your midst."*

Theologians have debated this for centuries. I wonder, though. Does it have to be one or the other? Can't it be both?

I think it can, and am happy to report that I am in good company. When considering the question "Is the Kingdom of God now or something we await in the future" Martin Luther responds "Yes" and "Yes!" Luther says in his *Large Catechism:*

> *"The kingdom of God comes to us in two different ways: first, in time, through the Word and faith; secondly, it will be revealed in eternity."*

If we insist that the Kingdom of God exists only in the future, then we sound rather self-serving. I behave now so that I can go to heaven some day when I die.

If Kingdom of God is NOW, how does that kingdom come about?

Well, friends, that's where we come in. Remember that loaded sentence from Jesus:

"Seek Ye first, the Kingdom of God?"

Seek ye means actively going after something. You don't just LOOK for it, you actively go after it by living a life to serve the Lord, all day, every day.

Think about it – there are in every year of your life - 364 opportunities (and sometimes 365) to work for the Kingdom of God.

That means WE are working toward that kingdom, FOR that kingdom, for building the Kingdom of God. We are the laborers.

How do we do this? This is a huge responsibility.

Your labor does not have to be a grand gesture. If you have a million dollars to donate to ending poverty in Africa, Great! Do it!

Building the Kingdom comes in everyday acts.

Here's an example: I was shopping in the infant department of a department store the other day, and noticed a woman near me pick up an item, look at it, stroke it lovingly, then put it back down and walk away. She had no idea I was watching her. Several more times she would return to the item, look it over, touch it and then walk away. When I got to the cashier the woman was nearby, holding the item, but still looking a little doubtful and maybe a little guilty. My interpretation was that the item probably was way outside her budget, but she really wanted to get it as a gift for a grandchild, maybe. I invited her over to the casher's counter and asked the clerk to please add her item to my bill. At first the woman protested, but, after some coaxing, she relented. A huge smile replaced the earlier look, and as we left the store together, she said "Thank you and God bless you. You have made my day."

Our Chancel Choir has a favorite anthem *Ain't Got Time to Die*. Some of its text goes like this:

*"I keep so busy working for the kingdom, ain't
got time to die; when I give it my all, I'm
working for the kingdom; when I'm feeding the
poor, I'm working for the kingdom."*

The text implies that working for the Kingdom is NOT an insular, singular act. It affects everything. The song continues:

*"The rocks are gonna' cry out 'Glory and Honor,
glory and honor, aint got time to die'."*

All of creation is affected by our work for the Kingdom of God. The rocks are gonna' cry out "Glory and honor!"

Have you nurtured a child today? Your working for the Kingdom!

Have you fed someone who is hungry? (Invite them to respond with you) You're working for the kingdom.

Have you sat with someone who is ill or alone? You're working for the kingdom

Have you helped to sing God's praises? You're working for the kingdom

Have you prayed for someone today? You're working for the kingdom

Consider this passage from *Sermon on the Mount: Devotions for Lent* by Dean Nadasny:

*"The Kingdom of God is organic; it grows like a
seed. The Kingdom of God is dynamic; it carries
its own power to change, renew and expand. The
Kingdom of God is inviting; it seeks and finds
new people. The Kingdom is now and not yet."*

Your work jobs may not always have a happy ending. Nadia Bolz-Weber in her book *Pastrix* says:

"Jesus brings a kingdom ruled by the crucified one and populated by the unclean and always found in the unexpected. The kingdom which Jesus talked about all the time, is, as He said, here. At hand. It's now. Wherever you are. In ways you'd never expect."

It's messy sometimes.

I had a friend, more of an acquaintance I guess, who for varied reasons began shunning me, criticizing, spreading nasty rumors, etc. After some months of this she descended into alcoholism, and in the depths of her depression called on me for help. Many times, I would stop by and counsel her, bring dinner, listen, reassure her. She wanted to reconnect with a church and I helped her do it. When her husband was hospitalized, I visited them. In one of her tearful rants, she asked "Why are you being so nice to me?" I responded, "We are all children of the same God." In the end, given the opportunity, she again betrayed me. We are now totally estranged.

Would I do anything differently, even though the ending was not a happy one? No. Why? Because we have been called, NOT to succeed, but to be faithful. God has called us to keep on building the kingdom. We can't always create the outcome. We just keep on working.

How do we know when our working is truly building up God's kingdom? We have a perfect model. Jesus.

"Jesus is an evolutionary paradigm."

Now there's a mouthful. An evolutionary paradigm. That should appeal to those scientific types. Evolutionary – developing into. Paradigm – a model or example. In other words, Jesus is the model for what we can develop into. So that movement from a few decades ago – *What Would Jesus Do?* – was not too far off the mark. We have a perfect model toward which we can evolve.

ALL THESE THINGS

So, if you work for the kingdom,

"All these things will be added unto you."

Do these things and you'll be wealthy. NO. We are not talking about "Prosperity theology" that promises wealth if you do certain things like donate lots of money to large churches.

Jesus emphasizes FIRST. Seek FIRST the kingdom of God, He says, and all these things will be added unto you. Sure, you provide for family, develop your profession, etc. But these things should not be your main focus. Besides they are all temporary. God doesn't want your THINGS. If we have trust that God provides for us, this leads to freedom from worries about finances and such. And because we are freed from those worries, we have more time to labor building God's kingdom. We are rich, not choked by riches.

Lord to whom shall we go?

RIGHTEOUSNESS

First in your life, seek the kingdom of God and His righteousness

Righteousness is defined as "the quality of being morally correct and justifiable." It can also be considered synonymous with "rightness". It is a concept that can be found in Indian religions and Abrahamic traditions as a theological concept. For example, from various perspectives in Hinduism, Christianity, and Judaism it is considered an attribute that implies that a person's actions are justified, and can have the connotation that the person has been "judged" or "reckoned" as leading a life that is pleasing to God.

In I Cor. 6:19 Paul says:

"Your body and your Spirit belong to God."

The Rev. Mike Winger goes on to say:

"So righteousness is a vessel for the Holy Spirit."

We are in a relationship with God. Because God is righteous, we are righteous. So then, due to this right relationship, "all these things shall be added unto you." All that is important will be in place for you.

FINALE

My husband and I chose this hymn "Seek Ye First" as our wedding processional.

The wedding guests sang it as we walked together down the aisle.

We see God's hand in our union. We see God rubbing God's hands together saying "Boy do I have a surprise for you?"

We don't work for the kingdom with that reward in mind, but boy do we love it when all good things are added unto us. We know we are blessed

Lord to whom shall we go? You have the words of eternal life. Seek Ye first the kingdom of God and His righteousness and all these things shall be added unto you. Thy kingdom come, Lord.

15

Ascension

June 6, 2019

First Presbyterian Church, Newark, DE

SCRIPTURE READINGS: Acts 1:9

Psalm 47

John:14-17

Dedicated to Charlotte French

It was a bright and beautiful Thursday in May a few years ago. My calendar showed no appointments or commitments. So, I decided to take a trip into Dutch country to explore, and to visit a favorite Amish market called Singing Springs. Not your ordinary market, it was used by the Amish themselves – no electricity, only generators. No fancy packaging, everything could be bought in bulk – oatmeal, flour, honey, home-baked products. I loved that market, especially to hear the customers speaking Pennsylvania German among themselves. I understood all of it, but they didn't know that. Such fun!!!

Enjoying the ride north toward Lancaster County, I came upon an Amish buggy also heading north. And then, after working around that one, fairly soon, another. You know, at first you think "How Charming; How quaint." And maybe you reflect on how wonderful it is to observe simpler times, a slower-paced lifestyle.

As I got deeper into Lancaster County, there were more buggies, and then more. No more charm and quaintness. Now they are downright annoying because I just couldn't get where I wanted to go. Why so many I thought. Where is everyone going?

Finally, I reached Singing Springs Market and immediately noticed something strange. The parking lot was empty. No Amish buggies. Very, very unusual. I parked and went up to the door of the market where a handwritten sign was taped to the glass. It read "Closed for Ascension."

I was crushed! Not because I was deprived of my shopping spree, but because it had never occurred to me that today was Ascension Day. Ascension Day - a very significant festival on the Christian calendar. I realized I had joined those who suffer from ADD, Ascension Deficit Disorder.

What about all those buggies we were passing on our way? They were going to church to celebrate Ascension, which, by the way is always on a Thursday 40 days after Easter.

You know those times when you're feeling proud - my prayer life, my spiritual life, my church life - I've got it all together. And then you come face-to-face with a circumstance, an occasion, a lesson such as this one demonstrated by a very humble, unprideful folk who were simply doing what they are called to do - being faithful.

Unfortunately, this is probably most often the case with Ascension. We don't think about it much. We rarely hold services to celebrate Ascension, especially not on a Thursday. It pales in comparison to other big festivals - the carols and decorated trees, angels and shepherds of Christmas, or the lilies and egg hunts and new dresses and chocolate-laden baskets at Easter. This is Ascension Sunday. How should we celebrate? Why should we pay attention at all?

Three good reasons: Ascension is exciting, it is important and it is absolutely essential. Let's explore those reasons for a bit.

EXCITING?

OK, imagine yourself as one of the disciples, the onlookers as Jesus ascended into heaven. St. Luke writes in Acts 1:9

"As they (the disciples) were looking on, He was lifted up, and a cloud took Him out of their sight."

Can you imagine how incredible, scary and amazing that must have been for those witnesses?

He was lifted up? Here we are 2000 years later and we know now that if you go up to find heaven you've got a long way to go. We know you go up and up and still further up and all you find is more UP.

I can't begin to explain it, but I have faith that it is true, because I know that God can do whatever God intends to do. If witnesses say that God took Jesus up, then so be it.

There was a cloud, Luke said, that took Jesus out of sight. The cloud IS significant. These ancient Hebrews interpreted the cloud as the presence of God. Remember the Israelites wandering in the desert toward the Promised Land? They were led by a pillar of fire at night and a cloud by day. God was leading their wandering. I believe there was a cloud, too, when Moses climbed Mt. Sinai to receive the 10 Commandments. (The first time a person downloaded data from the cloud onto a tablet.)

So, who would argue that there might have been a cloud in the vicinity of the Mount of Olives that enveloped Jesus, obscuring Him from view, and that this cloud was a manifestation of the divine presence?

Psalm 47 is the perfect choice for this festival day.

"Clap your hands all ye peoples, shout unto God with the voice of triumph. God has gone up with a shout, the Lord with the sound of the trumpet. Sing praises."

This is a song of enthronement. God is enthroned in the heavens. God is King. This is a song of triumph, a song of victory! These first Christians, though a small and endangered band, spread the Gospel with boldness. Christ's Ascension empowered them. God was KING!

Jesus' Ascension was exciting to watch . . .

BUT WHY IS IT *IMPORTANT* FOR US TODAY?

The Ascension marks a very important intersection in the life of the church. It is nothing less than the meeting of the Father, the Son and the Holy Spirit. It is the end of Jesus' earthly mission and the welcoming of Him, body, soul and spirit into heaven. God is there lifting Jesus up unto God's self. The Holy Spirit is poised to aid the disciples in continuing the Christian mission.

It is important to us because it shows us what is in store for us. Yes, we will rise from the dead, but then what? Through Jesus' Ascension God shows us that God will lift us up to be with God's self for all eternity.

I love the words from Acts "He (Jesus) was lifted up." To me that is so precious. We tenderly lift up a beloved child because that child is so cherished. God lifts us up to be with God because we are beloved, precious and cherished.

I'm a big fan of imagery. Can't you just envision God's hands enfolding His beloved children and drawing them to Himself?

I had a friend in seminary whose sister took her own life. My friend went to her pastor to seek comfort, because in her culture, suicide was an absolutely unforgiveable sin. Her pastor gave her wonderful counsel, words I will never forget. He said:

> *"There is nothing so low, so terrible, so awful,*
> *that the hands of God cannot reach under*
> *and lift it up."*

Are you feeling the lift?

NOW WHY IS THE ASCENSION ABSOLUTELY ESSENTIAL?

The history of Jesus Christ does not end with His death and resurrection. His disciples were eyewitnesses not only to His death and the empty tomb, but they also ate with the risen Christ, who repeated His promise to send the Holy Spirit to help them in *continuing their mission*. The Ascension of Jesus is the connecting event. It is as if, as He ascends, He passes the baton to His disciples.

It's as if Jesus is saying to them and to us, "I have shown you what to do, now go and do likewise."

The beautiful part of Jesus' leave-taking was that He prepared His disciples for it. Take some time to read John chapters 14 through 17. This is sometimes called the farewell discourse. So many verses that we know by heart are contained here. It is all about Jesus getting His followers prepared for *carrying on the mission* once He is gone.

> *"I am going to prepare a place for you. I wouldn't say it if it weren't true. My peace I leave with you. Love one another even as I have loved you. I will not leave you comfortless. I am with you even to the end of the age."*

These words of farewell were spoken to the disciples but they are also spoken for us. Jesus' followers witnessed His Ascension. They had to have been totally convinced that Jesus no longer walked the earth. Now they can fully understand that He intends them to continue His work – preaching, teaching, feeding the hungry. By acknowledging this Ascension, we too see that Jesus intends for us to do the work He demonstrated in His earthly mission. And Jesus' promise rings true.

> *"I am with you always, even to the end of the age."*

Jesus prayed for His disciples and prays for us. I like to imagine that, as Jesus prays in John:14–17, the disciples are nearby waiting and watching and, I think, eavesdropping. And further, I like to imagine Jesus wants them to hear, wants us to hear Him praying for us.

He says:

> "Father, they were yours; you gave them to me
> and they have obeyed your Word. I pray for
> them. I will remain in the world no longer, but
> they are still in the world. Please protect them
> by your Holy name. Sanctify them. I want them
> to be with me where I am."

Jesus lifted them up in prayer. Jesus lifts us up in prayer.
You feel the lift you want to share that gift.
The hymn *Go to the World* carries the message in wonderful poetry:

> "Go to the world, go into every place
> Go live the word of God's redeeming grace
> Go seek God's presence in each time and space.
> Go to the world; go struggle, bless, and pray
> The nights of tears give way to joyous day
> As servant church, you follow Christ's own way
> Go to the world; go as the ones I send
> For I am with you, till the age shall end
> When all the hosts of glory cry 'Amen.' "

✝

References

A Song in the Dark, Max Lucado

Bible Commentary, New International, F. F. Bruce, General Editor

Enduring Word Website

Evangelical Lutheran Worship (hymnal), Evangelical Lutheran Church of America, Augsburg Fortress Publishing, 2006.

Glory to God, (hymnal) Presbyterian Church USA, Westminster John Knox Press, 2013

Grace Notes: Hymns of the Lukewarm Church, February, 2000

The Bible in History, Thomas L. Thompson

Let There Be Light, (poem) Helen Needham

Life Application Bible, New International Version, Tyndale House Publishers, 1991.

Lutheran Book of Worship, (hymnal) Lutheran Church in America, Augsburg Publishing House, 1978

O Magazine, "Need a Lift?" Jessica Winter, 2009

Pastrix, Nadia Folz-Weber, Convergent Books

Preaching.com, "Jesus Christ: The Yoke's on You", Jim Shaddix

PSALMS (from the online series) Psalm 139; Ho Escape from God, Steven E. Cole

RCL/Narrative/Evangelio/Index, Commentary on Psalm 47, Nancy Koester

SermonCentral.com, "The Prodigal Sons," by Robert Leroe, Cliftondale Church, Saugus, MA, 6/7/13

Sermon on the Mount: Devotions for Lent, Dean Nadasdy, pub. Creative Communications for the Parish, 2014

Small Catechism, A Contemporary Translation, Martin Luther, Augsburg Fortress, 1991

Sundays and Seasons, Autumn, "Preaching the Season," 2000

Swallow's Nest, Marchiene Vroon Rienstra, Friendship Press, 1992

The Bible in History, Thomas L. Thompson

The Courage to Love, William Sloane Coffin, Harper & Rowe, 1982

The Living Psalms, Claus Westerman, pub. T. & T. Clark, 1989

The Parables of Jesus, Joachim Jeremias, pub. SCM Press, 2003

The Runaway Bunny, Margaret Wise Brown

Women's Bible Commentary: ed. Carol A. Newsom & Sharon H. Ringe, pub. Westminster John Knox Press, 1998

About the Author

Joanne Reitz Hench was born and raised in a Pennsylvania German farming village. The German Lutheran Church she attended as a youth was the center for her families' civic, social and spiritual activities. She credits that church with inspiring her, and offering her the opportunities and strong foundation for building a life-long career as a church music professional. Fluent in German, Joanne has acted as translator for various groups on her frequent visits to Europe, and has translated documents from German to English for the company Scholarly Resources. She holds Master's degrees in both music and religion and has recently retired after 60+ years as Music Director/Organist for a variety of churches. Joanne lives in Newark, Delaware with her husband. Together they boast 6 wonderful children, plus spouses, and 12 beautiful grandchildren.

Contact Joanne at jreitz53@gmail.com